"Vaneetha writes with creativity, biblical faithfulness, compelling style, and an experiential authenticity that draws other sufferers in. Here you will find both a tested life and a love for the sovereignty of a good and gracious God."

—JOHN PIPER, author of *Desiring God*;
founder and teacher, desiringGod.org

"*The Scars That Have Shaped Me* will make you weep and rejoice not just because it brims with authenticity and integrity, but because every page points you to the rest that is found in entrusting your life to one who is in complete control and is righteous, powerful, wise, and good in every way."

—PAUL TRIPP, pastor, author,
international conference speaker

"I could not put this book down, except to wipe my tears. Reading Vaneetha's testimony of God's kindness to her in pain was exactly what I needed; no doubt, many others will feel the same. *The Scars That Have Shaped Me* has ͪ ͥ me process my own grief and loss, and given me hope to care for those in my life who suffer in ways. Reveling in the sovereign grace of God will bolster your faith like nothing this worͪ Vaneetha knows how to lead you to this li

—GLORIA FURMAN ͬ ͣ*l*
Mother ͥ *Him*

"When we are suffering significantly, it's harᴅ ͤ eive truth from those who haven't been there. But Vaneetha Risner's credibility makes us willing to lean in and listen.

Her writing is built on her experience of deep pain, and in the midst of that her rugged determination to hold on to Christ."

—**NANCY GUTHRIE**, author of
Hearing Jesus Speak into Your Sorrow

"I have often wondered how Vaneetha Risner endures suffering with such amazing joy, grace, and perseverance. I still don't understand that, but this book has given me a new glimpse into her world and into the character of our loving God. Raw, transparent, terrifying, and yet amazingly hopeful, *The Scars That Have Shaped Me* can provide strength for the journey regardless of your situation."

—**BRIAN FIKKERT**, co-author of *When Helping Hurts: How to Alleviate Poverty Without Hurting the Poor . . . and Yourself*

"When I'm in a hard place and needing to draw deeply into God, I want to hear from someone who knows and understands. Someone who's been there. I can think of no better voice than Vaneetha Risner's. In both the sudden crisis and the long, relentless daily struggle, Vaneetha's insights have been purchased in the fire of adversity. So I listen. She leads through a door that comforts my soul and straightens my spine—I am in her debt. You will be, too, as you drink deeply the wisdom she has to offer."

—**PAULA RINEHART**, author of *Strong Women, Soft Hearts* and *Sex and the Soul of a Woman*

"In the unfathomable logic of God's wisdom, this faithful woman with increasingly weakening physical strength has, of all the people I know, the most secure grip on God's steadfast faithfulness and reliability. Her faith has helped me weather the storms in my own life, and the words in these pages will do the same for you. Vaneetha Risner is the real deal."

—**MARGOT STARBUCK**, author of *The Girl in the Orange Dress: Searching for a Father Who Does Not Fail*

"It's hard to find words to express how vitally important Vaneetha's testimony has been in the shaping of my life and faith. She has walked uniquely hard roads and ventured into deep spiritual waters, yet always welcomes fellow travelers like me. These pages are full of vulnerability and hope, rooted not in optimism but in the real-life experience of God's faithfulness in suffering. It is truly oxygen to get a glimpse of God's face through Vaneetha's eyes."

—**CHRISTA WELLS**, singer, songwriter

"In *The Scars That Have Shaped Me*, Vaneetha proves to be an able guide who can lead us through the valleys of tragedy and hardship with both grace and truth as she unveils the brilliant and redemptive power of God in the darkness of human misery. As her friend and pastor for many years, I can personally testify that the paths on which Vaneetha will lead the reader she has faithfully walked herself. She invites us all to see God's sovereign and good glory in times of testing and struggle."

—**TOM MERCER**, Senior Pastor, Christ Covenant Church, Raleigh

"*The Scars That Have Shaped Me* accomplishes the nearly impossible: Vaneetha tells her story of suffering—which has been, and still is, large—without drawing us into her pain. Instead, by grace and wisdom she guides us to find the way through our own sufferings into the heart of God. Somehow she lays out her story of gut-kicking suffering while captivating us with her experience of the goodness of God in the midst of her pain. The result? Our hearts are emboldened to trust and submit to Jesus. Her book is a gift to those who suffer, and to those who walk alongside them."

—SALLY BREEDLOVE, Spiritual Director, Cofounder of JourneyMates, Author and Speaker

Foreword by Joni Eareckson Tada

VANEETHA RENDALL RISNER

the Scars
that have
Shaped Me

HOW GOD
MEETS US
IN SUFFERING

The Scars That Have Shaped Me: How God Meets Us in Suffering

Published by Desiring God
2112 Broadway St NE, Suite 150
Minneapolis, Minnesota 55413

Print/PDF ISBN: 978-1539506584

Cover design: Amy Bristow

First printing 2016
Printed in the United States of America

To Shalini

Without you, not a chapter in this book would exist,
for you have pointed me to Christ in the darkest days,
encouraged me to record God's love and faithfulness, and
edited every word I've written.

CONTENTS

PART I: FEARFULLY AND WONDERFULLY MADE

You formed my inward parts; you knitted me together in my mother's womb. I praise you, for I am fearfully and wonderfully made. (Psalm 139:13–14)

PART II: LOOK ON MY AFFLICTION

Look on my affliction and deliver me, for I do not forget your law. (Psalm 119:153)

Why are you cast down, O my soul, and why are you in turmoil within me? (Psalm 42:5)

How long, O Lord? Will you forget me forever? How long will you hide your face from me? (Psalm 13:1)

I am afflicted and in pain; let your salvation, O God, set me on high! (Psalm 69:29)

I am in despair. I looked for pity, but there was none, and for comforters, but I found none. (Psalm 69:20)

PART III: JOY COMES
WITH THE MORNING

Weeping may tarry for the night, but joy comes with the morning. (Psalm 30:5)

FOREWORD

Joni Eareckson Tada

Before You Begin

Most people think that living with quadriplegia would be utterly overwhelming. And they're right. It is. Shortly after I broke my neck, I met a young man in rehab who told me he had been in a wheelchair for eight years. I gulped, pushing down the panic in my throat. To me, eight weeks of paralysis seemed impossible. But eight years?! It was unimaginable to me, a spinal-cord injured teenager who still retched at the thought of living life sitting down.

But that was decades ago. I can hardly believe I've been living without use of my hands or legs for almost 50 years. I still look back and wonder, *how did I make it to this point? And how have I done it, for the most part, with a smile?* Even after all this time, total paralysis still seems impossible.

But with God all things are possible. And whenever I try to explain how I have "arrived" at this point, I shake my head in amazement.

It has everything to do with God and his grace that sustains—not just over the long haul, but grace given in tiny moments, like stepping-stones leading you from one tick of the clock to the next. And the beauty of God's grace is that it squeezes those hard moments together, eclipsing the years until one day you look over your shoulder and all you see is five decades of God at work.

Try as you may, you cannot recall the horror of it all—grace softens the edges of past pains, choosing only the highlights of eternal importance. What you are left with is peace that's profound, joy that's unshakable, and faith that is ironclad. It is the hard but beautiful stuff of which God makes your life. *Like . . . when did* that *happen?* I cannot say, but I praise God for his amazing grace.

Vaneetha Risner would say the same. Here is a woman who understands deep suffering with its sorrows and joys. Perhaps that's why I consider her such a close friend. She gets it. She resonates with people in pain.

And she offers a special kind of wisdom to the reader in *The Scars That Have Shaped Me.* The book you hold in your hands is nothing short of remarkable. With each chapter, my friend tenderly turns over the stepping-stones of her own journey through suffering, helping us understand the hard but beautiful stuff in our *own* lives . . . how God meets us in *our* suffering . . . and how *we* are changed forever in it and through it.

One more thing. Vaneetha and I both recognize that vulnerability is so necessary in communicating a powerful story. But we also realize that our testimonies won't really reach—or even change—the life of the reader. Only the word of God can do that. And *The Scars That Have Shaped Me* is overflowing with snippets of psalms, slices of Scripture, and stories from the Bible that tell the story of God and his purposes in our pain. Vaneetha reminds us that God's reasons are perfect and that our Savior, intimately acquainted with grief and suffering, is constantly pleading our case before heaven's throne. What could be more comforting than that?

And so I am *honored* to write this opening statement for her book. For we both know that suffering is a strange, dark companion; but a companion, nonetheless. It's an unwelcome visitor; but still, a visitor. Affliction is a bruising of a blessing; but it *is* a blessing from the hand of God. It is how God meets us in our suffering.

I pray that *The Scars That Have Shaped Me* will inspire and refresh your heart—especially if *you* are in the midst of hardships or heartaches. So get started, turn the page, and be blessed by the story of Vaneetha Risner. Before you are through, you'll be looking over your own shoulder and seeing much more than pain and disappointment—you'll see the unmistakably hard but truly beautiful stuff God is doing in your own life.

JONI EARECKSON TADA
Joni and Friends International Disability Center

Agoura Hills, California

INTRODUCTION

I almost titled this book *He Makes My Griefs to Sing*,[1] because the phrase so beautifully describes what God can do in our suffering. But that could make me sound eloquent and poetic, when I am neither. And furthermore, I can't sing. Just ask anyone who has had the privilege of sitting near me in church.

So making my griefs to sing isn't pretty. Not only because I can't carry a tune and I have no idea what "pitch" is, but also because the song I sing in my grief doesn't sound winsome. It's often a desperate cry for help, not a stirring hallelujah chorus. But in the end, God has taken my griefs and turned them into something beautiful. He has indeed made my griefs to sing.

I am well acquainted with suffering. Many of you reading this book are as well, and suffering has carved hollows into your soul. Some of you may even feel abandoned by God, as trials have threatened to overwhelm you. I honestly have felt that way too, both as an unbeliever and as a committed Christian. I have been tempted to turn away from him in my pain, wondering why a good God would let his children suffer. Yet the Lord has proven abundantly faithful, as he has filled those hollow places with an overflowing joy. Leaning into Jesus, I have discovered that he alone is my greatest treasure and walking with him is my greatest joy.

I feel honored to publish this book with Desiring God, especially because the Lord used their ministry to transform my view of suffering. Almost twenty years ago, I heard a John Piper message on the sovereignty of God, and was immediately convicted by how man-centered and earthly-focused my view of life was. For the first time, I became aware of how God uses suffering and trials in the lives of believers for their good and his glory. Since nothing is outside of God's control, I realized that all of my experiences could deepen my eternal joy. The Lord knew that I would need this newfound perspective to sustain me, for suffering would continue to mark every decade of my life.

This book was borne out of that suffering. My story begins in India, where I was born to Christian parents. As an infant I contracted polio, long after it was virtually eradicated. Because the doctor had never seen polio before, she misdiagnosed me and prescribed the wrong treatment. Within a day, I was totally paralyzed. The physicians in India offered little hope for my recovery and encouraged my parents to seek better medical care in the West. We quickly moved to London, where I had my first surgery when I was two years old. By the age of thirteen, I had undergone twenty-one operations and had moved from England to Canada and finally to the United States.

I lived in and out of the hospital for most of my young life and learned to walk, albeit with a pronounced limp, at age seven. Though hospital life was lonely and isolating, I felt safe and "normal" when I was there. At home, I enjoyed the comfort of a loving family but was openly picked on at school. Feeling like an outcast, I wanted nothing to do with God because he had allowed all of this to happen. But when I was in high school, God met me in my bitterness and I committed my life to him.

I went out-of-state to college and then moved to Boston for my first job. Several years later, in graduate school, I met and married a classmate, and we soon had our first daughter, Katie. After three miscarriages, I was pregnant again with a son, whom we discovered would be born with a serious heart defect. Paul had a successful surgery at birth, but when he was two months old, he died as a result of a doctor's mistake. It was soon afterwards that I heard John Piper's sermon on God's sovereignty, which radically changed my perspective on suffering. A year later we had another daughter, Kristi, and I busied myself parenting two children, teaching a Bible study, and speaking on the comfort of God in the midst of loss.

Several years later, I developed an inexplicable pain in my arm and was eventually diagnosed with post-polio syndrome. This disease involves increasing pain and weakness, which could potentially result in quadriplegia. The most difficult part for me is that the more I do now, the less strength I will have for the future.

After years of adjusting to this new life filled with limitations, my husband decided to leave our family. Within a few weeks he had moved to another state and our once close-knit family collapsed. Parenting adolescent daughters amidst chaos and pain while striving to model grace proved beyond my ability. Yet it forced me to rely on Christ in ways I never had before. Although it was not my choice to divorce, we eventually did, and I was faced with trusting God for a new chapter of my life. A chapter, like others, that I didn't want to begin, but I knew would increase my dependence on God.

In time, God blessed me with a wonderful new husband, Joel, whom I married in 2015. Before I met Joel, I began writing a blog in late 2013 at the prompting of several friends. Writing was a way to remind myself of God's faithfulness. I then started posting articles for other ministries, excited that God would use my words to encourage fellow sufferers. This book is a compilation of some of those writings.

Though the book has a purposeful order, the individual chapters do not need to be read sequentially. The first section largely contains my life story; the middle section is centered on finding God in various trials; and the last section points to the blessings that God gives us in suffering.

I wrote this book for anyone who has experienced loss, particularly those who are struggling now. But I found that in the middle of a storm, I cannot read or process too much at one time. As such, each chapter is brief and can stand alone. I pray that the Lord will use these words to sustain those who are suffering, illuminating the priceless treasures God gives us in the darkest of places.

PART I:
FEARFULLY
AND
WONDERFULLY
MADE

*You formed my inward parts; you knitted me
together in my mother's womb. I praise you, for
I am fearfully and wonderfully made.
(Psalm 139:13-14)*

THE SCARS THAT
HAVE SHAPED ME

I've long despised my scars.

I have spent much of my life hiding them, keeping my legs covered as much as possible. My scars told me that I wasn't like everyone else. They told me I was unattractive, an oddity, a bit of a freak. Some people are proud of their scars; they speak of courage. They show others what they've endured. They carry with them stories of bravery and adventure.

But for me, with scars covering both my legs, they were not medals to display, proclaiming my bravery. They were rather deficiencies to hide, reminding me daily of my flaws—reminding me I was damaged.

As a teenager, I desperately wanted a perfect body, hoping that a perfect body would make me feel accepted. Instead, I saw in the mirror a body deformed by polio and further marked by the twenty-one ensuing operations. In a world filled with images of flawlessly photoshopped models, it was a challenge to believe that my physical imperfections were beautiful.

So hiding my scars was natural. That way, no one could see how imperfect I was. That way, I could look more normal. That way, I wouldn't be humiliated. *My scars were simply jagged reminders of my pain.*

I hated going to the pool, or the beach, or anywhere that my legs could be seen. Even if no one openly stared, I imagined that everyone was repelled by my scars. I assumed that if they saw the real me, I wouldn't be accepted. I was convinced that my scars made me ugly.

When Scars Speak

For a short while, a close high-school friend convinced me to show my legs at the beach. She said my scars might be ugly to me, but to everyone else, they represented strength and courage. To everyone else, they revealed what I had endured just to walk. To everyone else, they were just part of what I'd been through. And for a while, I did show my bare legs, but I slowly reverted back to covering them up. It was easier that way.

I went back to believing the lies I had told myself: I was more valuable if no one could see my scars.

I hid my wound marks and was comfortable doing so for decades. But one day, I noticed this in the Gospel of John: "Jesus came and stood among them and said to them, 'Peace be with you.' When he had said this, he showed them his hands and his side. Then the disciples were glad when they saw the Lord" (John 20:19b–20).

The disciples recognized Jesus when they saw his scars. And Thomas needed to feel the Lord's nail wounds to verify that the risen Savior was before him. Jesus didn't need to have scars on his resurrected body. His body could have been perfect, unblemished, unscarred. But he chose to keep his scars so his disciples could validate his identity. And even more importantly, so they could be assured that he had conquered death.

Michael Card's song, "Known by the Scars," expresses this truth so beautifully.

> The marks of death that God chose never
>   to erase
> The wounds of love's eternal war
> When the kingdom comes with its
>   perfected sons
> He will be known by the scars[2]

God chose not to erase these marks of death—the wounds of his love for us—so our Savior will always be known by his scars. Rather than physical imperfections, Jesus's scars are breathtakingly beautiful. They represent his love and our salvation.

The Places I've Been Healed

As I considered these truths, something stirred in me. My scars are significant and precious. I shouldn't keep hiding them. I am recognizable by them; they make me unique. They are an integral part of who I am. They show that, through Christ, I am a conqueror—that I have suffered and, by the power of the Holy Spirit, have overcome. My scars remind me that God is sufficient and that physical perfection is not our goal. A life lived to God's glory is infinitely more valuable.

Scars represent more than I ever realized. They can be beautiful. The dictionary says "a scar is a mark left by a healed wound."[3] *A healed wound*. My scars signify healing. And even though my initial flesh wounds have healed, there is yet a deeper healing in acceptance.

I started to notice scars more as I looked around. There was something captivating about people who were unafraid to be themselves: authentic, unmasked, and unashamed of the wounds that shaped them. Their vulnerability was magnetic. I was drawn to them. To learn from their self-acceptance. To hear their stories. To see their courage.

I learned it is often a good thing to ask people about their scars. As long as I do it respectfully. And lovingly. Asking demystifies scars and allows people to share what has shaped them. Because all scars have a story.

I saw that when we display our scars, we inspire others to do the same.

Those of us with scars should wear them like jewels, treasured reminders of what we've endured. It's okay to show our imperfections. It is even courageous. And perhaps we'll discover the beauty in our scars.

THE WOUNDS OF
BULLYING

"Cripple. You're a cripple. You don't belong here!" Seconds after I heard the jeers, I felt the sting of gravel hitting my back. It scattered along the path, and I heard a group of boys laughing. I looked up to see who they were, but they were hidden from view.

As the pelting continued, a short, heavy-set boy stepped out of the shadows. He laughed as he imitated my pronounced limp and lightly pushed me in contempt. I tried to maintain my balance, but within seconds, I collapsed on the pavement.

Immediately the boys dispersed and it was silent. The area was deserted. I was alone.

I sat there for a minute, fighting back the tears and trying to collect my thoughts. I didn't know who had done this, and I didn't know why, but I was ashamed. *Something was wrong with me.*

Since I couldn't get up easily without help, I waited to see if anyone would come by. Eventually, I dragged myself to a nearby rock and painstakingly hoisted myself up. Relieved that no one saw me, I picked up my books, pulled myself together, and began the short walk to my house.

I wasn't going to cry. I wasn't even going to look upset. I was going to be cheerful.

Determined to block out what had happened, I ignored my aching body as I trudged home. When I neared the front door, my mother ran outside, beaming. "Wow! You walked home without your sister for the first time. I'm so proud of you!"

"Yeah, me too," I said, forcing a smile.

After we went inside and my mother poured me a glass of milk, I offered, "I earned a sticker today . . ."

I never told her what happened that day. I was too embarrassed. I was just seven years old.

My Secret Pain

Sadly, this was not an isolated incident of childhood bullying. Throughout grade school, I endured different types of bullying. Some of it subtle. Some of it overt. All of it humiliating. And I never talked about any of it.

I had contracted polio as an infant in India before my vaccination date. Almost immediately afterward, we moved to the West for my medical care. I spent the majority of my young life in and out of the hospital. By age thirteen, I had undergone twenty-one operations.

Since I encountered cruelty so frequently, I almost came to expect it. No one ever stood up for me. Even when I was bullied in front of others, they looked the other way. They didn't want to get involved—and I didn't expect anything different.

Because I never told anyone about being harassed, I drew my own conclusions about what was happening. And over time, the power of those conclusions became magnified and deeply ingrained. I told myself that something was wrong with me. I was the outcast. I wasn't worthwhile. These insecurities became my invisible wounds.

I compensated well and learned to make friends, but inside I was always angry. That anger melted when I met Jesus at age sixteen after reading John 9. God showed me through Scripture that just like the man born blind, he was going to use my handicap for his glory. This revelation profoundly changed me as I saw my life through a new lens, one that was bigger than just my comfort.

I rarely thought about the bullying in my childhood until years later, when a painful rejection in my adult life triggered those emotions again. Although the situation was new, the feelings of inadequacy—of not measuring up, of being unimportant—felt strangely familiar. It was as though the flesh had been ripped off my invisible wounds, leaving me bloody and raw all over again.

Facing My Past

My feelings surprised me. I started journaling about my life in an effort to heal and sort out my emotions. As I wrote, long-buried memories came flooding back, carrying with them all the lies I had believed. The lie that my handicap made me subpar. That I wasn't intrinsically valuable. That I was defective.

I shared my story with a friend as I searched for understanding. I was hesitant at first, not sure if it would be too humiliating to tell someone. I was an adult, and bringing up the past seemed childish and pointless. Yet as my past came to the light, something started to change. The lies from my past ceased to hold the same power over me. I was not to blame for what had happened. What the bullies did and said to me wasn't really about me. It was about them.

I spent time in prayer, asking God to show me truth. I needed to know who I really was. He showed me the exquisite beauty of the gospel. I saw that I am not defined by what other people have said or done to me. I am defined by who I am in Christ. Jesus alone can tell me who I am. And he tells me that I am loved. Accepted. Of great worth.

I can see the way God has used the bullying in my life to shape me. Through those wounds, he has given me compassion, resilience, and grace. He is exchanging my ashes for beauty as he fulfills his life-changing promise to use my handicap for his glory.[4]

IS GOD REALLY THERE?

"God, if you are real, please show me."

He was desperate. In prison. Hopeless. His life was a mess and he figured he'd give God a chance. If God even existed, that is.

So he prayed. And waited. And looked for signs of God. There were no answers written on the sky. But slowly, God brought people and circumstances and books to open his eyes. A random cellmate reading a Christian book from Christian Library International passed it along. Which led to a Bible study. And a mentor through CLI. Soon he knew. Beyond any doubt. This God that he had heard about was indeed real. And had called him out of darkness into light. And his world would never be the same again.

As I listened to the speaker, now out of prison and serving in full-time ministry, I was both grateful and amazed. Grateful that God calls us through no merits of our own. And that he uses people and circumstances and ministries to show us his truth. Amazed that I had spoken those very words to God the night before he revealed himself to me. "God, if you are real, please show me."

Desperation

My story was quite different, but my words were spoken out of desperation as well. Life wasn't turning out the way

I wanted. My days seemed meaningless. My many questions felt unanswerable. God couldn't be real, I had assumed. I had given up believing in God a long time before. There was little evidence of him in my world. My life had been difficult.

After contracting polio as an infant, I spent much of my childhood in the hospital, isolated from my parents, my sister, and my peers. While hospital life was lonely, it was less painful than the constant bullying that I experienced in the real world. Nearly every day I heard the word *cripple*. Through elementary and middle school, I buried the hurt of that teasing deep, yet it constantly whispered to me that I didn't count, that I didn't belong, that I'd always be an outsider. I learned to stuff my feelings down, to please others, to be the good girl on the outside, while inside I was a self-absorbed mess.

Supplication

I grew up in the church, but I wanted nothing to do with this God I had heard about. But at the same time my life had no joy—just bitterness and anger. I knew something was missing. So one night, in the darkness, I cried out to Jesus. I wanted the issue settled. I wondered if God was even real. So I simply whispered, "God, if you are real, please show me." My question was sincere, and I waited for a response, some indication that I'd been heard. When nothing happened, I rolled over and fell sleep, my suspicions confirmed.

When I woke the next day, I wondered if I'd get an answer. I didn't expect to. But to cover my bases, I decided to read the Bible. Reaching over to my nightstand, I pulled out an unopened RSV translation that had sat there untouched for years.

Flipping aimlessly through the pages, I read whatever passages my eyes landed upon. They didn't make sense. As usual. Leviticus had weird rules and Chronicles had endless pages of names. I was about to put the Bible away, convinced that God indeed was not real, when I stopped to ask a question.

Illumination

"Why? Why did all of this happen to me? If you are so loving, why did I get polio? Why have I had to struggle my whole life? How can you possibly be good?" I thumbed through the Bible one last time looking for answers. It fell open to the Gospel of John and I began reading at John 9:

> As he passed by, he saw a man blind from his birth. And his disciples asked him, "Rabbi, who sinned, this man or his parents, that he was born blind?" Jesus answered, "It was not that this man sinned, or his parents, but that the works of God might be made manifest in him." (John 9:1–3 RSV)

Jesus's explanation was a little different than the disciples' question: they were focusing on the cause of this man's disability while Jesus spoke to the purpose behind it. According to Jesus, this wasn't a punishment or even random misfortune. It had been planned all along by God. Those words took my breath away. God was answering me. Arrogant, self-pitying, angry me was being answered by the God of the universe.

My suffering had a purpose: to bring glory to God. To some, those words may seem puzzling. Maybe even disturbing. But when they are spoken to you by the God of the universe, those words change everything. It was the most amazing moment of my life. I will never forget it. Even now, as I remember that morning, it brings me to tears. Just as God opened the eyes of a blind man to bring glory to himself, God was opening my eyes. For the first time, I could see him. Sense his presence. Understand he was real.

Salvation

I closed my Bible and knelt down by the side of my bed. As the sun streamed into my room, I committed my life to a God I didn't know but was certain knew me. He had created me for a purpose—to bring him glory. And all that I had endured in my life was to accomplish that end.

God, who knew me and each of us before the foundation of the world, calls us uniquely. Not based on anything we have done but based solely on his irresistible grace. And this call often begins with him answering a simple prayer. Not a theological or learned one. Just a sincere cry.

So if you don't know Jesus, would you consider praying, "God if you are real, please show me?"

And then look around to see how he is answering you.

BURYING A SON

Burying my baby was devastating. I had no idea how to cope with his sudden, unexpected death. True, Paul had been born with a heart problem, but he had survived the critical surgery at birth and was thriving. He'd come home from the hospital at three weeks old and, after a slow start, began gaining weight.

We had prayed so long and so hard for this precious child, I felt certain Paul's life would be used to glorify God. I couldn't wait to see how.

With his winsome smile, easy disposition, and mop of curly dark hair, he delighted us all. He was healthy and beautiful. Even the physician filling in for Paul's regular cardiologist was so impressed with Paul's progress that he decided to eliminate all of our son's heart medications. Paul didn't need them anymore. He was fine. At first, I was encouraged by the good news. But two days later, Paul was dead. He was only two months old.

I struggled to accept what had happened: that a doctor's foolish decision took our baby's life. As I watched them lower Paul's tiny casket, I buried my dreams for him. How could his life glorify God? I felt that nothing good could come from his pointless death.

I grieved. I journaled. I planted flowers that bloomed in the month of his birth and flowers that bloomed in the month of his death. Slowly, God healed me with his comforting presence, but still I wondered how God could be glorified through such a sudden and senseless death.

Held

Months later, I shared the story of Paul's life and death with a new friend, Christa Wells. Christa is a recording artist who subsequently wrote the song "Held," which begins with the story of Paul. The opening lyrics are raw:

> Two months is too little,
> They let him go
> They had no sudden healing
> To think that Providence
> Would take a child from his mother
> While she prays, is appalling

The chorus provides the response,

> This is what it means to be held
> How it feels when the sacred is torn from
> your life
> And you survive
> This is what it is to be loved and to know
> That the promise was when everything fell
> We'd be held.[5]

The words of the chorus echo my experience. God loves us. He holds us in our pain. And because of his love and compassion, we can go through anything knowing he'll never leave us.

"Held" was recorded by Natalie Grant in 2005 and won numerous awards and touched countless lives. As I read messages from people who felt God's comfort in their pain because of the song, I saw how Paul's short life had brought God glory. But none of the letters impacted me as much as seeing how it changed someone firsthand.

Touched

It had been a miserable, rainy day and I was feeling sorry for myself, running behind on errands because of the stormy weather. Partially drenched, I ducked into a bagel shop to grab a quick lunch. It wasn't busy, but the guy making my sandwich seemed interminably slow.

Couldn't he go a little faster? I wondered, as I sighed impatiently. He was almost finished, just tearing the final leaf of lettuce, when "Held" came on the radio. As I heard the familiar chords, I felt my tension and irritation roll away. Thankful for the delay, I smiled and leaned against the counter to enjoy the moment, unhurried. Something healing had come out of my brokenness, and it was still healing me.

Lost in my thoughts, I didn't notice that the young man making my sandwich had stopped. When I looked up, he was crying. Our eyes met and he apologetically mumbled, "I'm sorry. Are you in a hurry? Do you mind if I stop for a minute and listen to this song? You see, my mom died a few months ago, and this song is the only thing that got me through. It has meant so much to my whole family."

I cringed at my prior impatience. Pulling myself together, I nodded and whispered, "Please do. Take as much time as you want. I love this song, too."

Time stopped as this stranger and I shared a sacred moment together. I stood in silence as he took in the song, mouthing the familiar words as I recited them in my head. When the song was over, tears were streaming down my face as well. Tears of hope. And redemption.

Purpose in My Suffering

I knew the song had touched thousands of people, but I'd never seen evidence of that firsthand. I had never witnessed its healing impact on broken people. I had never fully understood the way God was using it to comfort others. I'll never forget that day. Seeing purpose in my suffering was more redemptive than I had ever imagined. While it didn't take away the pain, it did take away its sharp sting. Knowing that God was using my loss made it easier to endure. It helped me see how God uses all of our suffering for our joy and his glory.

None of my other trials have been memorialized with a song, but God has brought meaning to them all. With each loss, he has pulled me closer to himself and shown me the depth of his comfort. The deeper the sorrow, the more profoundly he draws near.

God has also met me as I talk to others who have experienced their own suffering. I'm often tempted to shy away from sharing because I don't want to relive the agony. It's often less painful to stay on the surface with struggling people. It's easier to remain detached. But inevitably when I do that, I leave emptier and more burdened.

I know how much it meant to me to talk to others who had walked similar paths. They were able to offer advice and insight; they understood the unique sorrows of my particular trial and they provided evidence that healing was indeed possible. In the pit, sometimes I doubted that. I wondered if I'd ever make it through. I questioned if the aching would ever stop. I wasn't sure if I would ever laugh again. Just talking to fellow sufferers gave me hope for the future.

God uses us to comfort one another with the comfort that we ourselves have received from God. It is both a privilege and a responsibility. And as we tell others of God's faithfulness in the midst of trial, it reminds us afresh that God will never forsake us. Though we may walk through the valley of the shadow of death, we will never walk alone.

MY FAILING BODY

I have always wanted to be self-sufficient. And I worked hard at it. I contracted polio as an infant in India and was left a quadriplegic after my fever subsided. But after several surgeries I was able to walk and, after additional operations, became fairly independent. By high school, I had learned to organize my life around my limitations.

Going away to college was another major hurdle, and I wondered how I would survive. To everyone's surprise, I learned to adapt, and by the time I graduated, I had figured out how to manage on my own. After a few years of work and then grad school, I got married and had children, grateful that the hardest part of my disability seemed behind me.

I was a typical stay-at-home mom, busy caring for my children. I also enjoyed painting, scrapbooking, and making jewelry—basically anything I could create with my hands. I started selling my jewelry at a local store, but soon afterward I developed an agonizing pain in my right arm. I went to the doctor, and after several months was diagnosed with post-polio syndrome. My arms would never recover. The doctors said I needed to reduce the strain on them. Immediately. Radically. Permanently.

I was told post-polio was a degenerative condition that results in escalating weakness and pain. My energy was like a fixed sum of money in a bank—I could make withdrawals but not deposits. So every time I used that arm, I was losing future strength. From now on, my energy could not be spent on short-term hobbies: I needed to focus on being able to feed myself long-term. Now my arms could only be used for absolute essentials.

This diagnosis blindsided me, turning my comfortable life upside down. I was a thirty-seven-year-old wife and mother with two young children to raise. It was unthinkable I could one day—maybe soon—be in a wheelchair full-time, unable to care for myself. *How could God do this to me?* I wept. How could I handle these new obstacles?

Devastating Losses

I stopped scrapbooking and boxed up my roomful of supplies. I gave up painting and making jewelry and canceled my subscriptions to cooking magazines. I made simple meals and entertained less. While all of these losses were difficult, losing my independence was the most excruciating. I constantly had to ask for help doing everyday tasks—things I longed to do for myself.

For me, the loss of self-sufficiency was humiliating. I hated being dependent on other people. But I had no choice. I started to need help driving long distances, making dinner, and occasionally even getting dressed. I had long defined myself as a helper, and I struggled with this role-reversal. I didn't want to have needs; I wanted to be needed. I didn't want to be a burden; I wanted to lift others' burdens. I didn't want to be dependent; I wanted to be self-sufficient. Every day I fought against asking for help. I desperately wanted to do things for myself. And I cried constantly. It seemed unfair that ordinarily easy, everyday tasks were now exhausting for me.

At first I was angry. Then I grew depressed. I didn't know if I could accept this new life. I pulled away from God. I questioned his goodness and his love for me and figured he wasn't going to answer my prayers, anyway. But eventually I realized I could not face this trial without God. I finally poured out my heart to him and asked him to help me handle my losses well. To show me how joyful my dependence could look. To give me grace to deal with whatever I was given.

And God changed everything. Not by changing my circumstances but by lighting a path through the darkness. He taught me how to pray, how to ask, and how to receive. He gave me glimpses of his glory. He showed me how he is using my circumstances to change me.

The Daily Battle

It was a constant struggle. And if I'm completely honest, it is *still* a struggle. I think it always will be. Part of me will always long for my independence. But in that longing, I have learned to lean on God in prayer. I have learned how to offer God my honest lament—my anger and grief poured out unedited. I have learned to tell God what's hard and admit that I dread asking for help. I have learned that prayer changes my perspective on my life. Through prayer, I am reminded that heaven is real and one day I will have a new body.

Until then, I need the humility to ask for help. Asking for help is always hard because I'm proud and I'd rather not need anyone. But most people are more than willing to help—they are just waiting to be asked. Sometimes people can't help, and in those situations I must graciously accept that without getting discouraged and without giving up. The first person I ask is not always the person God has chosen to help.

Glimpses of Glory

The entire process is humbling, but this dependence on God and on others has grown my faith in incalculable ways. Second Corinthians 4:16–17 says, "So we do not lose heart. Though our outer self is wasting away, our inner self is being renewed day by day. For this light momentary affliction is preparing for us an eternal weight of glory beyond all comparison." Though my strength is declining, my faith is growing stronger, and one day I will see what he has done with my suffering.

I can show the surpassing worth of Christ when I suffer well—when I joyfully accept circumstances that are less than perfect, when I give up my need to control. Willingly relinquishing my need to have things exactly as I want is an act of worship.

My faith and my character are not all that has grown through my losses. My friendships and sense of community have deepened tremendously as well. I have been humbled and amazed at the willingness of others to help, even at great cost to themselves. I see the love of Christ in how he cares for me through the body of Christ. As my physical body is deteriorating, his body has taken over for mine, showering me with love and unexpected kindness. Kindness I would have never known if I hadn't needed it.

Love I would never have experienced if I had refused to ask for help.

As I depend on Jesus more and more, he is gradually transforming me into his likeness. There's no one I'd rather depend on; there's no one I'd rather look like.[6]

A CRUMBLED MARRIAGE

I've survived some devastating storms. Contracting polio as an infant, living in the hospital for years, being bullied in grade school, enduring four heartbreaking miscarriages, and burying a beloved infant son have steeled me for almost anything. But the hurricane that ripped through my life several years ago left me more terrified and bewildered than I'd ever been, threatening to destroy my very foundation.

In my late thirties, I was diagnosed with post-polio syndrome, a debilitating disease marked by pain and escalating weakness. The doctors told me I needed to give up my hobbies and focus on the essentials. If I didn't, they said, in ten years I'd be in a wheelchair full-time, unable even to feed myself.

I pared my activity down to the bare minimum, daily assessing how much I should do. It was achingly hard, especially with two young daughters. But slowly, I learned to adjust. Then six years later, as profound weakness was setting in, my husband of seventeen years left our family unexpectedly. Within two weeks he moved to another state.

Depths of Darkness

His leaving plunged me into the darkest time of my life. Friends brought meals and helped me care for my homeschooled daughters while I spiraled into the dark. I lost ten pounds in a few weeks, staying in bed for days without eating, pulling the covers over my head, hoping it was all a bad dream. But as the days wore on, the reality of it set in. I was a single mom with two adolescent daughters.

My girls were understandably angry, taking out their fears and frustrations at home. Our once peaceful home turned into a war zone, with rage and disappointment coloring every conversation. They decided they wanted nothing more to do with "my" God and wondered if he was even real. I cried myself to sleep every night, often whispering from my bed, "God, do you still love me?" Sometimes I screamed in the darkness, "God, why do you hate me?" I kept thinking that the worst was over, but each day seemed to bring more pain.

A Troubling Passage

One night, in desperation, I picked up my Bible and started randomly paging through the Gospels. I needed a fresh encounter with Jesus. I stopped at John 11, the raising of Lazarus, and I reread the familiar account.

> Now a certain man was ill, Lazarus of Bethany, the village of Mary and her sister Martha. . . . So the sisters sent to him, saying, "Lord, he whom you love is ill."

But when Jesus heard it he said, "This illness does not lead to death. It is for the glory of God, so that the Son of God may be glorified through it." Now Jesus loved Martha and her sister and Lazarus. So, when he heard that Lazarus was ill, he stayed two days longer in the place where he was. (John 11:1–6)

Every time I read these words, they catch me. How could Jesus love Mary, Martha, and Lazarus and still delay? If he loved them, he could have gone immediately. He didn't need to let Lazarus die. But that's what happened.

Jesus's response reminded me of the ways he was letting me suffer. For months I had been begging God for deliverance. And for months there had been silence—just as with Lazarus. Jesus could have gone to his friend, or simply said the word, and Lazarus would have been healed. But Jesus didn't do *anything*.

I started sobbing as I realized this was the crux of my pain. Jesus could fix all of my struggles in an instant. He could heal my body, bring my husband back, and change my children's hearts. But he wasn't doing anything. I felt as though he had abandoned me, just as he had Lazarus and his sisters.

The Bible says that Jesus loved his friends, so he delayed. But in my thinking, love rescues. Love runs to help. Love responds. Love doesn't delay.

Seeking in the Darkness

I wanted to understand this passage. It made no sense to me. And later in John 11:40, what does Jesus mean when he tells Martha, "Did I not tell you that if you believed you would see the glory of God?"

God promises to show Moses his glory in Exodus 33, and he makes good on that promise a few verses later, in Exodus 34, *by speaking of his own attributes.* "The Lord, the Lord, a God merciful and gracious, slow to anger, and abounding in steadfast love and faithfulness, keeping steadfast love for thousands, forgiving iniquity and transgression and sin" (Ex. 34:6–7).

A greater understanding of who God *is*, what God is *like*, what he *does*—*that* was God's revealed glory, not a brilliant flash of light or some undefined ecstasy. And Moses's response to this glory was worship. This is the first time the Bible records Moses's spontaneous, personal worship. And after that encounter, Moses's face shone. He had changed. Moses was different.

In my pain, I cried out to God, "I want to see you, and I want to believe that you are for me. I believe, help me to overcome my unbelief. Show me your glory."

Then I waited. In silence. For a long time.

God's Presence Revealed

I pondered what I had prayed and read. As I did, I saw God afresh through the lens of Scripture, and immediately his presence seemed to fill my room. Seeing God's glory was so simple yet so profound. He is merciful and gracious. Slow to anger. Abounding in steadfast love and faithfulness. Those attributes were not just intellectual. They were specifically directed toward me.

God was speaking to me. Just as with Moses, God was revealing who he is. God loved me enough *not* to rescue me. He knew I needed to see him, to sense his presence, to understand his heart. I needed those things more than I needed rescue. There will always be something new to be rescued from, but this encounter with God will stay with me forever.

Jesus loved Mary, Martha, and Lazarus enough to show them his glory so they could be transformed. He loved them enough to let them suffer so they could experience his comfort. He loved them enough to delay his coming so they could learn to walk by faith. Seeing his glory led Mary to offer her extravagant worship, pouring out expensive perfume on Jesus's feet. My "seeing" led me to worship, too. Jesus seemed nearer than he had ever been, more tender than I had ever understood, and more glorious than I ever imagined.

More of Jesus

We all need more of Jesus. One moment with him changes us just as it changed Mary, Martha, and Moses. The shift from wailing to worship has nothing to do with changing circumstances; it is *we* who are changed by encountering God, seeing his goodness and power, understanding his character.

This experience led me to worship, it grounded me in ways I cannot explain, and it transformed me forever. Jesus said, "Did I not tell you that if you believed you would see the glory of God?" (John 11:40).

And seeing his glory is a far greater gift than rescue.[7]

PART II: LOOK ON MY AFFLICTION

Look on my affliction and deliver me,
for I do not forget your law.
(Psalm 119:153)

LAMENT: BEAUTY
FROM BITTERNESS

When pain almost strangles us and darkness is our closest friend, what should we do?

For years, I thought the best response was cheerful acceptance. Since God uses everything for our good and his glory, I felt the most God-honoring attitude was to appear joyful all the time. Even when I was confused and angry. Even when my heart was breaking. And especially when I was around people who didn't know Christ.

But I have since learned the beauty of lamenting in my suffering. Lament highlights the gospel more than stoicism ever could. Hearing our authentic lament can draw others to God in unexpected ways. I first noticed the power of lament in the book of Ruth.

Naomi's Trust in God

I had long seen Ruth as the undisputed hero of the book that bears her name, and Naomi as the grumbling character with weak faith and a negative attitude. But having walked in similar shoes for a fraction of her journey, I have a new respect for the depth of Naomi's trust in God. Ruth was an eyewitness to Naomi's faith. She saw that faith hold fast, even in horrific circumstances. And behind it she saw the God who heard Naomi's lament and didn't condemn her for it, even as Naomi spoke frankly about her disappointment with God.

Lamenting to a god would have been foreign to Ruth. Ruth's first god, the god of Moab, was Chemosh. No one would have dared lament or complain to him. Pagan gods were appeased; there was no personal relationship with any of them, especially not with Chemosh, who demanded child sacrifices.

But Ruth sees a completely different God as she watches Naomi. Naomi trusts God enough to tell him how she feels. Though she says, "the hand of the Lord has gone out against me" (Ruth 1:13), Naomi doesn't walk away from God in anger. She stays close to him and continues to use his covenant name, Yahweh, asking him to bless her daughters-in-law. Naomi doesn't stop praying; she believes that God hears her prayers.

Naomi's trust is further evidenced by her determination to travel to Bethlehem alone. If Naomi felt that God had truly abandoned her, she would never have begun that journey. She would have stayed in bed, pulled the covers over her head, and died in Moab, bitter and angry at God. But she doesn't do that. She acts in faith, trusting that God will provide for her.

Naomi's trust is extraordinary given the tragedies she has endured. She and her husband had left Israel for Moab with their two sons in search of food. While they were there, her sons and husband died and she was left alone. A widow. A grieving mother. A foreigner. With no means to support herself. I understand why she felt that the Lord's hand had gone out against her. In my own pain I have cried out to God, "Why do you hate me?" I have retraced my life, wondering why God had turned against me.

Naomi's Honesty with God

But to my regret, I've always been very private about my pain. I have hesitated to voice my anger and fears, concerned about what others might think. Lament can be messy, and I want my life to look neat. And I foolishly think my bleached prayers somehow make God look better. Yet Naomi is achingly honest. When she goes back to her hometown, she doesn't pretend everything is fine. She doesn't cram her pain into a closet and shut the door. Rather, she invites others to peer into the dark corners of her bitterness and frustration. She asserts that God has dealt bitterly with her and has brought calamity upon her. She admits that she is empty.

Her words may have made the townspeople uncomfortable. Laments often do. But her humility and utter honesty would have also drawn people to her. They could grieve with her. And they could grieve their own losses, too, without fearing God's disapproval or the judgment of others. Naomi's words are raw, but she speaks truthfully about God. She acknowledges that he is in control of all things and everything is ultimately from him. Her theology is profoundly God-centered. Underlying Naomi's lament is a deep trust and understanding of God. She is not resentful of God and has not turned away from him. Quite the opposite, Naomi is moving toward God with honesty. She has returned to Bethlehem, to the people of God, and is realistically presenting what happened to her.

Lamenting That Glorifies God

And it is in the midst of Naomi's pain and lament that Ruth comes to know God. Ruth gives up everything to follow Naomi and her God, whom she has come to know personally as Yahweh. She sees his faithfulness through Naomi, a woman who has experienced unspeakable tragedy yet continues to follow God, talking to him honestly and authentically. This is a God worthy of worship. Our authenticity draws others to God as it allows them to be honest, too. God welcomes our lament to help us hold on to him. He knows that our tendency is either to pretend everything is okay (while we suffocate on the inside) or to walk away from God, believing he doesn't care.

Lamenting keeps us engaged with God. When we lament, we invite God into our pain so that we can know his comfort, and others can see that our faith is real. Our faith is not a façade we erect to convince ourselves and others that pain doesn't hurt—it is an oak tree that can withstand the storms of doubt and pain in our lives, and grow stronger through them.

Godly lament does not repel people from the gospel but rather draws them to the Lord; it strengthens rather than destroys the faith of others. When we live authentically, we naturally draw others to God's grace. Naomi's pain and bitterness could have pushed Ruth away from God, as Ruth saw Naomi struggle with God's goodness. But instead, Ruth saw that Naomi's hope—even through catastrophic loss—was in a sovereign God who was loving enough to hear and respond to her lament.

And we can see that God did hear Naomi's lament and respond to it. He gave her Ruth. He gave her Boaz. He gave her a grandson, Obed, who was in the line of Christ. And he gave her himself, for that is what her heart needed most.

CRYING OUT TO GOD

I don't like to lament. It seems unspiritual.

Faithful Christians are even-tempered and cheerful. They rejoice in the Lord at all times. Without even a hint of discouragement. Even in difficult circumstances, they are unflappable. Nothing gets them down. Or at least that's what I've always told myself.

But when life falls apart, I find it almost impossible to rejoice. Instead, I wonder why God is allowing yet another trial into my life. I even doubt God's love for me. I feel sad at everything I've lost and dissatisfied with what I've gained in its place. I wonder if life will ever get better. Or if God has abandoned me indefinitely.

When Life Stops Making Sense

I used to respond by actively refocusing my mind, determined to have a positive attitude. But doing so left me even emptier and unhappier than before. Then I realized that Scripture never mandates that we constantly act upbeat. God wants us to come to him in truth. And so the Bible doesn't whitewash the raw emotions of its writers as they cry out to God in anguish, fear, and frustration when life ceases to make sense. People like Jeremiah and Job, Habakkuk and David have all poured out their honest feelings of sadness and disappointment to God.

- Jeremiah protests to God, "Why is my pain unceasing, and my wound incurable, refusing to be healed? Will you be to me like a deceitful brook, like waters that fail?" (Jer. 15:18)

- Job complains, "I will not restrain my mouth; I will speak in the anguish of my spirit; I will complain in the bitterness of my soul. . . . Then you scare me with dreams and terrify me with visions, so that I would choose strangling and death rather than my bones. I loathe my life." (Job 7:11, 14–16)

- Habakkuk mourns, "O Lord, how long shall I cry for help, and you will not hear? Or cry to you, 'Violence!' and you will not save?" (Hab. 1:2)

- David laments throughout the Psalms, modelling authenticity with God. In Psalm 13:1–2 he cries, "How long, O Lord? Will you forget me forever? How long will you hide your face from me? How long must I take counsel in my soul and have sorrow in my heart all the day?" In Psalm 22:1–2 he laments, "My God, my God, why have you forsaken me? Why are you so far from saving me, from the words of my groaning? O my God, I cry by day, but you do not answer, and by night, but I find no rest."

The Bible is shockingly honest. And because of that, I can be honest as well. I can both complain and cry, knowing that God can handle anything I say. The Lord wants me to talk to him, to pour out my heart and my thoughts unedited because he knows them already.

Navigating Grief

This conversation is different than the grumbling of the children of Israel. They complained *about* God and Moses *to* each other. I am talking directly to God. Telling him my doubts. Asking him to help me see. These saints I quoted all talked directly to God, which was the first step to healing. They named their disappointments and voiced their struggles before him. They needed to know that God understood them. And that they could be truthful with him. No pretense or platitudes. Just raw honesty, acknowledging their pain before God.

This process was essential to navigating their grief. And it is for me as well. When I don't acknowledge my pain, my lips may say one thing, but my heart says another. I start to wall off my heart so I can conjure up joy. But those walls make me numb to real emotion, unable to experience either pleasure or pain. My life flatlines as I start existing without really living.

Part of really living is being willing to face sadness. Not wallowing in my pain and refusing to be comforted, but honestly and openly telling God where I am and asking him to show me truth. Letting him, the God of all comfort, comfort me. Letting him, the God of hope, fill me with hope. And letting him, the man of sorrows acquainted with grief, bear my sorrows for me.

A Deeper Place

Pouring out my heart to God changes me. Like my biblical companions David, Habakkuk, Job, and Jeremiah, I can experience true joy only after I have acknowledged my sorrow. And when I do, I find myself in a deeper place with the Lord, who helps me reframe my disappointments and pain.

- David ultimately says in those very Psalms of lament, "I will sing to the Lord, because he has dealt bountifully with me" (Ps. 13:6) and "The afflicted shall eat and be satisfied; those who seek him shall praise the Lord!" (Ps. 22:26)

- Habakkuk acknowledges that his hope is in God alone as he declares, "Though the fig tree should not blossom, nor fruit be on the vines . . . yet I will rejoice in the Lord; I will take joy in the God of my salvation." (Hab. 3: 17–18)

- Job admits after his encounter with God, "I know that you can do all things, and that no purpose of yours can be thwarted." (Job 42:2)

- And Jeremiah sees that trusting our unfailing God changes us as he affirms, "Blessed is the man who trusts in the Lord, whose trust is the Lord." (Jer. 17:7)

The truth that emerges from our lips after we lament with the Lord is God-infused. We learn to trust God even when we cannot understand our own heartaches. I have seen this demonstrated in my own life again and again. It is most evident in my journals, where I unashamedly express my deepest feelings to God. The joyful praises with prayers of thanksgiving. The bitter disappointments mixed with anger and doubt. I have asked God why he doesn't love me, and I have heard him whisper through Scripture that he has loved me with an everlasting love.

As I write and pray, I sense his movement in my life. He comforts me. He fills me with hope. He bears my sorrows.

It's okay to lament. It's biblical. And when I pour out my heart to God in prayer, he does not rebuke me. Rather, he surrounds me. He puts my feet on a rock. He becomes "a shield about me, my glory, and the lifter of my head" (Ps. 3:3).

HAS GOD FORGOTTEN ME?

Some days are harder than others. Some mornings I can be cheerful even in the midst of difficult circumstances, and other days those same problems overwhelm me. Some days I wake up full of faith, and other days I doubt if God cares at all.

Invisible and Unmistakable

It was one of those difficult mornings when discouragement was almost suffocating me. I knew I needed something to revive me, so I opened the Bible to Psalms, my go-to book for lament. I am comforted by the psalmists' willingness to put their pain before God—raw and unfiltered—and let him handle it. I read Psalm 77, a Psalm of Asaph when he is desperate.

> I cry aloud to God . . . and he will hear me. . . .
> My soul refuses to be comforted. . . . Has God
> forgotten to be gracious? . . . Then I said, ... I
> will ponder all your work, and meditate on your
> mighty deeds. . . . You are the God who works
> wonders. . . . Your way was through the sea, your

path through the great waters; yet your footprints were unseen. (Ps. 77: 1–2, 9–10, 12, 14, 19)

I pondered the last line long and hard: "yet your footprints
were unseen." Asaph is remembering a time when God
guided the children of Israel though they couldn't see him.
And yet their deliverance was so miraculous, so extraordinary, so impossible, that only God could have done it.

I need to remember my own stories. They are unmistakable evidences of God. Times when the Lord has
helped me. The Bible calls them Ebenezers (1 Sam. 7:12).
Stones that remind us of God's presence, his help, his
faithfulness. The Israelites frequently gathered these stones
of remembrance, affirming their victory was the result of
divine assistance, not human strength. Remembering the
past gave them hope for the future.

My Ebenezer Board

I actually have an Ebenezer board. I made this board at
the suggestion of a spiritual mentor. We were talking
about spiritual markers. Pivotal moments. Encounters with
God. She gave me a basket of shells to use as my "stones
of remembrance," naming each one I found significant. I
sat and prayed, asking God to remind me of specific times
when I was changed by an encounter with him.

My first shell symbolized my conversion. When I
came to Christ at age sixteen, Jesus turned my life upside
down. Months later, my Fellowship of Christian Athletes
leader said that God used the disciples' radical commit-
ment to turn the world upside down. I wanted God to use
my life that way, too. I named my first shell Upside Down.

I was drawn to a starfish as my next marker, which began with hearing a sermon by John Piper on the sovereignty of God. As I listened to it, I had the profound sense that God was about to change my life forever. Piper talked about serving God out of delight, not duty. That day I asked God to give me a passionate desire for him above all things. I named this shell Delight and placed it beside the first.

A conch shell caught my attention for my next Ebenezer, a life-changing answer to prayer. A prayer I had whispered for a decade. A request that I had begun seeking God for daily—prostrate, face in the carpet, in my study. I was desperate. Just as the centurion told Jesus to say the word and his servant would be healed, I asked Jesus to just say the word. He did. And my world was forever changed. This shell I called Blessed be the Name.

I picked out two more shells, both representing unmistakable encounters with God. I can remember where I was and what was happening when I sensed God speaking to me. After each of those times, I was profoundly transformed. Later, I mounted all of these shells on a foam board and wrote the meaning beside each one. My Ebenezer board.

The Common Thread

So today, I pull out the board and run my fingers across the shells. Seeing them buoys my faith. Just like the Israelites, remembering the deeds of the Lord makes me grateful for his provision in the past. It gives me courage to trust him in the present. It gives me hope for the future. I am thankful as I look at this board. But as I stare at the shells,

I realize they have something in common: suffering. The times when I encountered God and sensed his presence were all borne out of pain.

My conversion occurred after sixteen years of dealing with polio. Sixteen years of being angry at God, wondering what I had done to deserve my handicap. The night before my conversion, I wondered if there was any purpose to my suffering. As I read John 9 the next day, I discovered the answer.

I heard the sermon about delight just weeks after I buried my son, Paul. I was wrestling in my faith, wondering why I had been singled out for such suffering. Wondering why my son had to die. Wondering if God even cared. Piper asserted in his sermon that God is in all our suffering, and he uses it all. This was radical, yet strangely comforting to me as I struggled to make sense of Paul's death.

The jaw-dropping answer to prayer commemorated by my third shell arose from a difficult situation, too. One I had sought the Lord about for years, alternating between hopelessness and anger. I was tired of waiting. I had often wondered if he would ever answer.

The other two shells have similar threads, as well. At first this troubles me. Why are all my markers related to pain? Why were my life-changing moments with God connected to suffering? Does God meet everyone this way? I look at Psalm 77 again. Asaph was recalling the parting of the Red Sea. A miraculous deliverance from the oppression of slavery. And in the moments before the miracle, the children of Israel were desperately afraid. They stood between Pharaoh's army and the water. There was no human way out.

My Low Points Are My High Points

I'm starting to see the connection, trying to piece this all together. It seems counterintuitive that the high points of my relationship with God would be connected to the low points in my circumstances. But the ways of God are often not what I expect. Perhaps only when I am truly desperate can I hear the Lord's still, small voice. Perhaps suffering and sorrow are God's invitation to know him better. Perhaps, as Laura Story says, the "trials of this life—the rain, the storms, the hardest nights—are [God's] mercies in disguise."[8]

So yes, God is working in every corner of my messy life. No, God has not forgotten to be gracious. Though his footprints are unseen, they are unmistakable.

TALKING MYSELF THROUGH SUFFERING

I can't carry my plate to the table.

Not long ago, I could do it easily. But with post-polio, my health is constantly deteriorating. Every week, I face new challenges, discover things I can no longer do, give up more things I love. The doctors told me this would happen. But as a young mother, there were other things to worry about. I assumed the real struggle would be decades away. Back then I could easily talk about it, write about it, and even philosophize about it. But now, as it's happening, I'm angry.

I sit at the counter, tears streaming down my face, flooded with emotion. I scream into my empty house, "God, how could you do this to me? Don't you love me? I've been faithful. Doesn't that count for something? Why don't you fix this?" Then I finish my tantrum with God and sink into self-pity. I decide that God answers other people's prayers but not mine. That he is unconcerned about my pain. That my suffering is meaningless.

Of course, these are the lies of Satan. I wish I didn't listen to them or know them by heart or repeat them almost instinctively. I wish, in the heat of battle when life is falling apart, my first response would be grace-filled. Patient. Christlike. I wish that I would savor the sweetness of God's sustaining grace and never question him again. But unfortunately I'm not there. Not yet.

So I close my eyes and breathe deeply. I need to repent. To heed Martyn Lloyd-Jones's advice: To stop listening to myself and start talking. On the back of an envelope, I jot down what I need to remind myself of. Seven principles that put suffering into perspective. Seven things I must do, even as I cry.

1. *Remember that God loves me.* I know how deeply the Father loves Jesus—and Jesus loves me that same way. Unconditionally, relentlessly, passionately. Nothing can separate me from God's love. The cross is a blazing reminder of it. Jesus is always for me. He sympathizes with me in my weakness. He understands my suffering. He weeps with me in my pain. He will never fail me or forsake me. He strengthens me when I'm weak. He calls me by name. He constantly intercedes for me. These are not merely intellectual truths. They are practical realities. Jesus knows what is hard, witnesses every heartache I endure, discerns the fears I can't even voice. He is with me as I sob. He waits for me to embrace him. He holds me in my pain.

2. *Talk to God.* I need his help, his perspective, his comfort. Intellectually knowing that this affliction is for my good is not enough; I need an encounter with the living God. And when I unreservedly pour out my heart to him, he tenderly meets me. When I feel desperate, my prayers are not long or eloquent. Sometimes they're just groans gasped out between sobs. Sometimes simple cries of, "Help me Jesus." Sometimes just silence before him. My biggest challenge is

not to turn away. Or stew in my anger. Or numb the pain elsewhere.

3. *Open the Bible and start reading it.* I often resist this straight-to-the-text approach; it can seem so academic. But as I open the Bible's pages, God speaks to me, whispering his comfort, shouting his promises, showing his grace through his inspired writers—people who were brutally honest about their suffering. They mentor me, modeling that it's acceptable to lament. To voice my frustration. To express my raw emotion.

4. *Remind myself that I am never alone in my suffering.* In addition to our triune God, I am surrounded by a glorious cloud of witnesses who see every struggle I experience (Heb. 12:1). While invisible to me, they are part of the spiritual realm, like the chariots of fire that Gehazi beheld (2 Kings 6:8–23). The unseen world. This world is real. And ever watching. Watching to see whether God is my treasure. Whether I will still praise him as my body deteriorates. Whether I will trust him when all looks dark.

5. *Recite God's faithfulness.* I have a record of my spiritual highlights, my unmistakable encounters with God, my Ebenezers (1 Sam. 7:12). The times when God has rescued me. Surprised me with joy. Overwhelmed me with his presence. When I am suffering, I need to review this list. It assures me that this trial will one day pass, but God's faithfulness and love will never fail. Often I reread old journals, seeing what I have agonized over in the past and then remembering how God sustained me through it. It

reminds me that he is trustworthy and will never leave me desolate.

6. *Set my mind on heaven.* This world is not my home and it is passing away. It will be over in the blink of an eye. And then real life will begin. Life with no more tears or death or crying or pain. The Bible constantly reminds us that our present sufferings must be viewed in light of eternity. Romans 8:18 says, "I consider that the sufferings of this present time are not worth comparing with the glory that is to be revealed to us." Even when life on earth seems relentlessly hard, God has all of eternity to lavish his love on us.

7. *Remember that this life is all about God.* Everything was created to make much of him whose ways are higher than my ways. I may not understand how, but God is doing something bigger with my life than I can possibly see. My suffering is never senseless; it will not be wasted. He will ultimately use every struggle for my good and his glory.

As I review these truths, I sense God's overwhelming peace. He will walk me through this trial, as he has every other one, patiently bearing with my weakness, lovingly speaking through his word, consistently giving me strength. These truths remind me that God loves me fiercely, cares for me tenderly, has purpose in my pain, and will one day make all things new. I am comforted knowing that my suffering now is not worth comparing with the weight of glory to come:

So we do not lose heart. Though our outer self is wasting away, our inner self is being renewed day by day. For this light momentary affliction is preparing for us an eternal weight of glory beyond all comparison, as we look not to the things that are seen but to the things that are unseen. For the things that are seen are transient, but the things that are unseen are eternal.
(2 Cor. 4:16–18)

*Why are you cast down, O my soul, and
why are you in turmoil within me?
(Psalm 42:5)*

HOW TO PRAY WHEN LIFE FALLS APART

In the midst of broken dreams and riveting pain, how should we pray?

Should we pray for healing and deliverance, believing that we just need to ask because God can do anything? Or should we relinquish our desires to God, trusting that even in our anguish he has the perfect plan for us?

Yes. When life falls apart, God invites us to do both. In the garden of Gethsemane, Jesus faced unimaginable suffering. Sweating drops of blood, he fell to the ground and prayed: "Abba, Father, all things are possible for you. Remove this cup from me. Yet not what I will, but what you will" (Mark 14:36). Jesus, in his agony, is teaching us by example how to pray when we're desperate.

Abba, Father

Jesus does not begin with, "almighty God, Maker of heaven and earth." Of course, God is Lord of all and deserves honor and reverence. But Jesus chooses a term of endearment: *Abba*. While *Abba* does not mean Daddy, it was used as an intimate, personal term for Father. Jesus is asking his Father to do something for him.

I grew up calling my father Daddy, and still do to this day. It was a great name when I was happy with him, but when I was upset I wanted to call him Sir. I could feel distant and defiant on the inside when I said "Sir," but there was no separating myself from him when I said "Daddy." And my father, who wisely knew this, insisted that I call him Daddy after our disagreements. When I was able to use that name sincerely, he knew our reconciliation was complete.

In a similar way, I need to draw near to God in my pain. He's the Almighty Lord, but he's also my Abba Father (Rom. 8:15). I need to approach him as such.

Nothing Too Difficult

Jesus knows God can do anything. He owns the cattle on a thousand hills (Ps. 50:10). All things are his servants (Ps. 119:91). Nothing is impossible with him (Luke 1:37). While I know those Scripture verses by heart, I often functionally doubt God's ability to change my situation. I scan my circumstances and assume things will continue as they are. Even as I'm praying, I don't look for miraculous answers; my prayers become rote recitations of requests more than earnest petitions of faith.

But in Gethsemane, Jesus *knows* his Father can grant his request. God gives life to the dead and summons into being things that don't exist. And I need to remember his limitless power when my situation looks insurmountable.

Remove This Cup

The cup Jesus asks God to remove isn't mere physical suffering. Disciples and martyrs through the ages have faced physical pain without fear. Jesus is anguished over suffering that's infinitely deeper. He is facing the terrifying fury of God's wrath over our sin. And he's facing that wrath alone, with no comfort from above.

Jesus knows God can change this horrifying situation. So he asks. He wants God to remove the very suffering he was sent to bear, the suffering he willingly came for, the suffering that would secure salvation for his people. Jesus wasn't coerced onto the cross. He laid down his life of his own accord (John 10:18). But now Jesus is asking if there is another way—any other way—for God to accomplish his purposes.

So often I filter my requests. Should I ask God to relieve my suffering when I know he can use it? Is it okay to ask for healing, or is that presumptuous? Should I not ask for anything and just accept what I've been given? That posture seems more holy.

Yet Jesus asks God to *remove* the cup. If Jesus can ask, I can, too. It's appropriate to ask God to remove my suffering, change my situation, keep me from further pain. He longs to give me good gifts. I've begged God to heal friends, save family members, and give clarity, and he has answered yes. But I've also pleaded with God to save my dying son, heal my escalating disease, and bring back my husband, and he said no. So even though I don't know how he will answer, my Father still bids me to petition him earnestly for the things I desire.

Not My Will, But Yours

Jesus finally relinquishes his will to God's. When denied his desire, Jesus accepts the decision completely. He stumbles to his execution without murmur or complaint.

This kind of relinquishment isn't easy for me. When I keep God at a distance, I can stay detached, without expectations. But if I draw near to him, even when I truly believe he can change the situation, I may nevertheless start to clutch at the outcome *I want*. I might verbalize "Your will be done," but I'm white-knuckling my own will. God often has to pry my fingers off my desired outcome. I've often been devastated when he tells me no, but as I submit to his will in those situations—even with disappointment and tears—he assures me he's working for my good.

I see only part of the picture. He has a purpose in his denials.

The Father said no to the Son. And that no brought about the greatest good in all of history. God is not capricious. If he says no to our requests, he has a reason—perhaps ten thousand. We may never know the reasons in this life, but one day we'll see them all. For now, we must trust that his refusals are always his mercies to us.

Run to Your Father

And now as we wait, still struggling to make sense of the storms in our lives, let us pray as our Savior did. Let us draw near to God, believe he can change our situation, boldly ask him for what we need, and submit our will to his.

Our Father's plans are always perfect. They will always be for our good and his glory.

WHEN DISAPPOINTMENT COMES

The news was completely unexpected. And upsetting. As soon as I heard it, my heart started pounding and a cold chill swept through my body. I couldn't believe this was happening. Shocked and disappointed, I immediately asked God for mercy. And the grace to respond well.

When I had time to calm down and think, I asked God to fix the situation—more accurately, I asked him to make it go away. I didn't want to face this problem and felt sick at what might lie ahead. I wanted God to take it away, make it "right," prevent me from suffering. I wanted the route that would make it easiest for me.

Why Me?

And then came my third response. I'm least proud of it. I thought: *Why me? Why do hard things always happen to me? Things were getting better, but now they are getting worse again. My life is filled with disappointment and pain, but I shouldn't be surprised. Nothing ever turns out well for me.*

I am ashamed as I write those words. Ashamed that I so easily fall into self-pity. Ashamed that I conveniently forget God's extravagant blessings. Ashamed at how quick I am to complain. I am no different than the children of Israel who remembered Egypt as perfect, yet saw the circumstances after their deliverance as intolerable. I whine to God that my life is harder than other people's. I assume everyone else has perfect health. Fulfilling lives. Conflict-free relationships. Successful careers. Thriving children. Insignificant problems. In short, I overestimate my problems and minimize other people's struggles.

For a little perspective, this disappointing news was not life-altering. It was difficult to hear, but not insurmountable. Although in the long-term it would be an insignificant event, in the moment it was all-consuming.

So in the midst of my pity party, I call my sister. She is my rock and my reality check. She keeps me grounded and reminds me of truth when I forget it. When I start ranting about how difficult my life is, she listens. She agrees it's a hard situation. But then I start spiraling downward, demanding, "Why me? Why is my life harder than everyone else's?"

She pauses to choose her words carefully. "I know it's incredibly difficult right now. And I will be praying continually for you. But don't believe that your life is always harder than everyone else's. Life is hard. For everyone. You don't always know what other people are going through."

I sigh as I lean back in my chair. She's right, of course. Her words remind me of the quote on my door: "Be Kind. For everyone you meet is fighting a battle you know nothing about."[9] We all struggle. Worry about our children. Have hard days. Face disappointment. Feel inadequate. Make mistakes we wish we could erase.

Start Talking

After I get off the phone with my sister, I remember Martyn Lloyd-Jones's words, "Have you realized that most of your unhappiness in life is due to the fact that you are listening to yourself instead of talking to yourself?"[10] And so I start talking. I remind myself of all of the extravagant blessings the Lord has poured out on me. The personal blessings, such as my loving husband and my supportive family. And the uniquely Christian ones that are lavished on all believers, such as redemption, the forgiveness of sins, the indwelling Holy Spirit, and the promise of eternal life. We are given all of this, along with countless other assurances, from the Bible. Assurances like, "For those who love God all things work together for good, for those who are called according to his purpose" (Rom. 8:28). Romans 8 helps me see that there is a bigger picture. I don't see the full plan. I can only see today.

Remembering Romans puts my life in perspective. God is not surprised by disappointing news. He knows it all beforehand and uses it to conform me into his image. As I reflect on the situation and the character of God, my prayer changes. I am able to say: "Though I don't understand this situation, Lord, you have brought it into my life. Because of that, I know it is good. And I know that you will use it—both for my good and for your glory. I want to trust you. Help me to do that."

Then, every time I think about the situation, I decide to seek God in it. Rather than dwelling on the negative, I begin praying that God will use it—in my life, for others involved, to his glory. This is not an easy prayer. It is a deliberate choice to push worry, anger, and self-pity away. But as I seek the Lord and keep talking to him, he enables me to take my thoughts captive. Slowly, my sense of desperation dissipates.

Recognizing that God is going to use this trial makes me calmer. So every time I think about the issue, rather than getting upset and anxious, I pray. I ask God to work in the situation. To redirect my emotions. To help me trust him. It's easy for me to jump to conclusions. To think that a trying situation is going to lead to another and then another. I often extrapolate present difficulties into the future—which is the crux of not trusting God. Those difficulties may never present themselves, but even if they do, God's grace will be there to meet me. Even if the worst happens, God will not fail me.

I wish I could remember these truths when problems first arise. I needlessly worry when I could be trusting God. I shouldn't be surprised when trials come. The Bible says to expect them. They train me and refine me. They do deep work in my soul. They reveal my character.

I do not know how this situation will end, but I do know that God brings beauty from ashes. No matter what happens, I know he will use it for my good and his glory. There cannot be a better ending than that.

WHEN THE DETOUR BECOMES THE NEW ROAD

This isn't the ticket I bought. That's what I thought when my health took a detour and I found myself on a road I hadn't anticipated. A road I wasn't prepared for. A road I didn't want to travel.

Laura Story understands how that feels. Everything radically changed after her husband was diagnosed with a brain tumor. Watching him struggle to breathe and cope with significant memory loss, Laura begged God to heal her husband and restore their lives to the way they had been. Life hadn't been perfect, but it had been good. Laura told her sister of her desire to return to the normal, trial-free life she had enjoyed before. And her sister insightfully responded, "You know, Laura, I think the detour you are on is actually the road."[11]

The detour you are on is actually the road. What a horrifying thought.

Aching for Normalcy

When my plans go awry, I always want to believe that I have taken a temporary detour. Maybe it's a long one, but I hope that the real road, the road where I can return to being happy and fulfilled, is just ahead. Maybe it's only around the corner, if I can simply hang on.

I was talking to a friend recently about that desire to return to normalcy. She doesn't know how to handle her newly developed health problems. Should she pray for healing and expect God to answer? Or should she come to terms with chronic pain and disability?

I understand her questions. I have asked them myself. Should I earnestly ask God to change my circumstances? Should I draw near to him in prayer, write down my requests, and regularly seek him for the things in my life that I want to see changed? Godly things. Restoration. Healing. Return to active ministry. Or do I recognize that I am on a different road? One that may not bring the healing and restoration that I would like, but rather a closeness to Jesus that I could not get any other way. Do I hold loosely to the expectation of changed circumstances and cling tighter to the hope that will never disappoint—the hope that is rooted in Jesus?

Yes.

God invites me to ask him to change the things that I long to be different. He invites me to persevere. To trust that my prayers make a difference. But at the same time, God bids me to accept where I am. To let him meet me in the darkness. To find comfort in his presence. To see him as more important than any change in my circumstances. God calls me to do both. Every day. On every road.

Adjusting to a New Normal

The old road often seems like it was more relaxing and easy to drive. The new road can be bumpy and twisty, nar-

row with sharp curves. And I find myself longing for the
ease of what I used to have. But the new road has benefits
too, perhaps not in ease but in seeing life differently. More
reflectively. Really noticing reality rather than rushing
forward, oblivious to my surroundings.

But regardless of what I gain, it's a challenge to accept
that the detour is now the new road. I struggle with that
reality daily as I experience new weakness and pain with
post-polio. Sometimes it's temporary, but often it's permanent. The loss becomes the new normal. And I must adjust.

Last month, I was going into a familiar building
when I realized I couldn't climb the curb without assistance. Without other options, I reluctantly asked a pass-
erby for help. She was warm and gracious as she helped
me and we had an encouraging conversation walking in
together. Since then I have been unable to get up sidewalks
without assistance. This limitation will change where I am
able to go by myself, requiring me to plan ahead. To be
honest, I don't want to plan ahead. I don't like limitations.
And yet, like my sweet conversation with a stranger, I'm
sure the Lord has unexpected blessings along this path.

I realize that I cannot cling to the past. I cannot get
back on the old road and put everything back the way it
was. Some things will get better over time. Some prayers
will be miraculously answered. Some dreams will come
true. But the old road is gone. And in my mind, it will
often be remembered as better than it actually was. The
Israelites did that when they complained after they were
delivered from slavery saying, "We remember the fish we
ate in Egypt that cost nothing, the cucumbers, the melons,
the leeks, the onions, and the garlic. But now our strength
is dried up, and there is nothing at all but this manna to

look at" (Num. 11:5–6). The Israelites neglected to mention that even though they had food, they were slaves. Their lives in Egypt were not perfect. They had continually cried out to God to deliver them from slavery.

Not Looking Back

So don't look back on the past and assume it was perfect. It wasn't. Mine wasn't perfect, either. This new road that I am on, bumpy and twisty as it may be, is the path God has chosen for me. It is the best road. The only one worth taking. If I keep looking back on the old way longingly, focusing on what I've lost rather than on what I have, I will miss the rewards of the new path. I need to open my eyes. Notice what's around me. Remember that God goes before me. I need not fear for he knows what is up ahead.

As he has promised, "I will lead the blind in a way that they do not know, in paths that they have not known I will guide them. I will turn the darkness before them into light, the rough places into level ground. These are the things I do, and I do not forsake them" (Isa. 42:16). God is guiding me on this new path.

I am on the right road. And so are you.

SHATTERED DREAMS
AND SHAKEN FAITH

Sometimes my faith is shaken when my dreams are shattered. I wonder where God is in the midst of my suffering. I cannot sense his presence. I feel alone and afraid. My faith wavers. I question what I have long believed. I wonder what is real, especially when my present experience doesn't match my expectations.

This wavering deeply troubles me. I have tasted God's goodness, enjoyed close fellowship with him, rested in his tender care. I have known both his power and his love. Yet in the midst of profound struggle, I have no answers. Just questions.

John the Baptist understood this struggle as he waited in prison. He, above all men, knew who Jesus was. Even in the womb, he leapt for joy in the presence of the unborn Savior. At the beginning of Jesus's ministry, before any of his miracles, John declared, "Behold, the Lamb of God, who takes away the sin of the world!" (John 1:29). He baptized Jesus and saw God's Spirit descend on him, testifying that Jesus is indeed the Son of God.

And yet, at the height of Jesus's ministry, John sent word to him from prison, asking, "Are you the one who is to come, or shall we look for another?" (Matt. 11:2–3). At one point, John was sure that Jesus was the Messiah. Jesus further confirmed his divinity by performing miracles, yet now John was wondering what was true. Why?

Unfulfilled Expectations

John knew from Scripture that he who gave the blind sight, made the lame walk, and preached good news to the poor could surely opening "the prison to those who are bound" as prophesied in Isaiah 61:1. But Jesus didn't do that for John.

So perhaps at this point, John doubted what he knew. If Jesus was indeed the Messiah, John probably expected to have a role in his earthly kingdom. He wouldn't have expected to start with such a high calling—preparing the way of the Lord in the wilderness—only to end his life and his ministry in a small prison cell. Besides, John preached that the Messiah would come with an unquenchable fire. With judgment. With power. He likely expected that to be in his lifetime.

None of those expectations coincided with reality. And that may have caused John to doubt. Unfulfilled expectations often elicit that response in me, especially when I've been faithful. Yet Jesus doesn't condemn John for his doubts. He even says that no one greater than John had ever lived. He understands why John is asking the question. And Jesus's response to him reinforces what John already knows: Jesus is indeed the Messiah.

At the same time, Jesus knows that John's public ministry is over. Just like the saints in Hebrews 11, John wouldn't receive all God's promises but could only greet them from afar. He would not serve with Jesus on earth or see the fulfillment of God's kingdom. But one day he would. One day he would see his glorious part in God's magnificent plan. He, the last of the old covenant prophets, would see how God used him to prepare the world to receive Jesus. And John would rejoice.

But for now, John has to accept the Messiah's plans for his life. Plans that are different than what he envisioned. He has to dwell on what he knows to be true rather than fixate on his circumstances. He has to remember who God is and trust him from a dark prison.

And so it is with me.

John's Doubts and Mine

When my plans crumble and God takes me away from my dreams, I must trust in God's infinite wisdom. When my cup of suffering seems too much to bear, I need to rest in his immeasurable love. When my life spins out of control, I need to remember God's absolute sovereignty.

I may not understand what is happening. But I cannot stop talking to him. Or turn away in fear. I must simply go to Jesus and tell him my doubts. Ask him to help me see.

John's doubts are the same as mine. I wonder if God is who he says he is. And if everything is under his control. And if he truly loves me. And when I doubt, God calls me, as he did John, to trust what I know to be true. To trust the bedrock principles I know from Scripture and from experience—that God is completely sovereign and loving and wise. Not a sparrow falls to the ground apart from his will.

In this life, I may never see how God is using my trials. But one day I will be grateful for them. All I can do now is trust that he who made the lame walk and the blind see, who died on a cross so I could spend eternity with him, is going to do the very best thing for me.

It all comes down to trust. Will I trust my circumstances that constantly change? Or will I trust God who is unchanging?

On Christ the solid rock I stand. All other ground is sinking sand.[12]

How long, O Lord? Will you forget me forever?
How long will you hide your face from me?
(Psalm 13:1)

THE AGONY OF WAITING

Waiting can be agonizing.

It's hardest to wait when I am uncertain about the outcome, when I'm trusting God for the best while preparing for the worst. It would be much easier if I had a guaranteed good outcome. Or at least a specific promise from God to hold onto, some reassurance to anchor my prayers. But God often seems silent when I'm waiting. I have no idea whether he'll ever answer my prayer, so it feels like I'm waiting in the dark.

I have read and reread Psalm 13:1–2, "How long, O Lord? Will you forget me forever? How long will you hide your face from me? How long must I take counsel in my soul and have sorrow in my heart all the day?" *O Lord, how long?*

I have asked that question many times. If I knew God would eventually answer my prayer with a yes, it would be different. But without such assurance, even a no would often be easier than "Wait."

When God Says No

Several years ago, I searched the Bible to find a promise that would help me in the midst of a torturous wait. I wanted a word that I could "claim." A verse that would assure me of eventual satisfaction. Something, anything, to cling to. As I was waiting, I read, "No unbelief made [Abraham] waver concerning the promise of God, but he grew strong in his faith as he gave glory to God, fully convinced that God was able to do what he had promised" (Rom. 4:20–21).

While I admire Abraham's faith, this passage often frustrated me. Of course Abraham never wavered. He had a direct word from God. If I had a direct promise from God, an assurance of my answer, then I'd be content to wait, too. Abraham could wait because he knew he'd get what he wanted in the end. I wanted God to give me a promise like the one he had given Abraham. So I kept begging God for a sign.

None came. No verse. No confirmation. Just silence on that issue. For years. And in the end, God's answer was no.

At first it felt unfair. And purposeless. I struggled to make sense of those seemingly wasted years. While I had grown closer to God, somehow I felt that I had received a lesser gift. I put it out of my mind after a while. It was senseless to keep dwelling on it. But whenever I read that passage in Romans, it stung. Why didn't God tell me his answer from the beginning?

One Model for Waiting Well

Several years later, as I begin reading Romans again in my quiet time, I hesitate at Romans 4. It painfully reminds me of that time of asking and waiting. Feeling disconnected from Abraham, I decide to look at his life in Genesis. I see Abraham's humanity as he sometimes doubted God's protection. He even tried to fulfill God's promise on his own through Hagar. Perhaps he thought God needed his help and ingenuity.

This part I can identify with. Abraham's struggle with impatience feels all too familiar. Too many times I've tried to help God fulfill his plans—that is, the plans I'd like him to have. Plans that would give me what I want. What I think I deserve.

As I study Genesis, I see that while Abraham was waiting, God was working. Molding his character. Teaching him patience. Building their friendship. It was in that twenty-five-year wait that Abraham got to know God intimately. It was in those seemingly wasted years that God transformed him. And after decades of waiting, Abraham was ready for the supreme test of his faith, when he was asked to sacrifice Isaac, the son of promise. The son he had waited for.

Then I see it. Why had I not noticed this before? Abraham's faith wasn't rooted in the promise of descendants. If it was, he never would have taken Isaac to be sacrificed. He wouldn't have relinquished what God had promised him years earlier. He would have clung tightly to Isaac, feeling entitled to this son. For Isaac was the fulfillment of God's long-awaited promise to Abraham. Abraham wasn't clinging to his own understanding of the fulfillment of God's promise. God could fulfill his promise any way he chose, including raising Isaac from the dead if he needed to (Heb. 11:19). So ultimately Abraham's faith lay in the trustworthiness of God.

The Most Precious Answer

Abraham's faith wasn't in the promise alone. His faith was rooted in the Promisor.

Because his faith was not in what God would do for him, but in God himself, Abraham was willing to risk. He could do whatever God asked. He wasn't holding on to a particular outcome. He was holding on to God. Abraham's waiting strengthened his faith. Taught him God's ways. Showed him God's faithfulness. *Abraham knew that God would provide everything he needed.*

I have the same assurance Abraham did—that God will provide everything I need. As I let that promise sink in, I see my waiting differently. Perhaps God is making me—and you—wait for the same reasons that he made Abraham wait: to forge our faith. To make us attentive to his voice. To deepen our relationship. To solidify our trust. To prepare us for ministry. To transform us into his likeness.

In retrospect, I realize that this is the most precious answer God can give us: wait. It makes us cling to *him* rather than to an outcome. God knows what I need; I do not. He sees the future; I cannot. His perspective is eternal; mine is not. He will give me what is best for me *when* it is best for me. As Paul Tripp says, "Waiting is not just about what I get at the end of the wait, but about who I become as I wait."[13]

BEGGING GOD

Once, in the middle of giving a talk, I almost broke down.
As I was recounting how I had begged God to save the
life of my son, I felt my chest tighten. I remembered how
desperate I felt. How sure I was that my begging would be
effective. How much I wanted to compel God to do what I
had asked.

After all, he is God. Nothing is impossible for him. I
had never wanted anything so much in my life, and it was
almost inconceivable that God would say no to such an
earnest request.

But God did say no. Even as I was pleading for my
son's life, he was dying. How does a good God let that
happen? I couldn't understand that. And I remembered
vividly many other times I had begged God for things that
he had refused me. As a child, I begged God to heal me.
In my twenties, I begged God to repair a broken romantic
relationship. And several years ago, I begged God to bring
my husband back.

Theology and the Holy Spirit

I wondered even as I was speaking, "Why doesn't God
answer my deepest prayers?" Of course, I had thought
through my theology before delivering my message. My
talk was about finding God in the middle of our mess. The

point of my talk was that God uses all things in our lives for our joy and his glory.

As I was saying the words "I begged God," I was flooded with the emotions I had felt decades earlier. Once again, I felt the raw pain of begging God and wondering why he had not answered me the way I wanted. At the time, I had felt abandoned. At the time, it seemed as though God didn't care at all.

But as I was speaking, the Holy Spirit met me. He used the words I was saying, and had written days earlier, to minister to me in that moment. He reminded me of the truth that while he always hears and answers our prayers, his answers may look wholly different from what we expect. And even as he gives us painful struggles to endure, he carries us through them.

I was addressing a group of women, many of whom had known extraordinary hardship. As I was talking, I was thankful for my own suffering, even if it wasn't as profound as some of theirs. My words were not phrases I had read in a book, but honest words that I had lived. In my own life, I have been much more moved by hearing someone's experience with God than hearing them recite facts about God.

His Refusals Are His Mercies

At the end of my talk, I had an overwhelming sense of God's purpose. I was overcome by a love for Christ and a joy in what he had done in my life. And in that roomful of women who had suffered so much, his presence was tangible. There were tears and repentance. There was hope and a renewed love for Jesus. I was standing on holy ground, grateful and amazed to be witnessing this profound work of the Spirit.

As I listened to these precious accounts, I saw a tiny glimpse of the glorious work God is doing in all of us. I saw that his refusals are his mercies; they had shaped me. Every answer of no drove me deeper into the heart of God, deeper into his word, deeper into prayer.

I was thankful for each "no," each trial and hardship, each affliction that drove me to my knees.

In my finite wisdom, I would never have chosen the path I have walked. It has been hard and gritty, and none of my struggles has had simple, happy endings, tied up neatly with a bow. But as I listened to these women's stories, I realized that God had chiseled and hammered me, said "no" when I begged for "yes," and offered his presence when I wanted his presents—because he had a much bigger plan for me. Part of it was telling people about his goodness in the midst of suffering.

I am thankful that I do not decide my future. God does. Left to myself, my journey would have been smooth sailing in spiritually shallow waters. My life would have been filled with temporary pleasures and perpetual emptiness. So today, when I think back over the instances when God said no, despite my begging, I am thankful. Though some refusals have left an ache in my soul, I would not seek to reverse them—in part because I often see purpose in them, but more importantly because I know that he will always do what is best for me. Even when I don't understand why, I trust that God has a purpose in my pain.

In *Walking with God through Pain and Suffering*, Tim Keller quotes John Newton saying:

All shall work together for good; everything is needful that he sends; nothing can be needful that he withholds. . . . Yield to his prescriptions, and fight against every thought that would represent it as desirable to be permitted to choose for yourself. When you cannot see your way, be satisfied that he is your leader.[14]

Everything is needful that he sends. Nothing can be needful that he withholds.

God knows what I need and has chosen for me what I would not have chosen for myself, given my limited perspective on life and my penchant for my own comfort. But if I had God's perspective and knew what he knows, I would undoubtedly choose what he has given me.

It has all been necessary.

UNFULFILLED LONGINGS

I was lonely for years. I longed to remarry, but I didn't want to admit it to anyone. Not even to myself.

I didn't want to pin my hopes on something that might never happen. And if I never remarried, I didn't want to look like I had wasted my life, hadn't trusted God, and couldn't be content. I'd be pitied by others and embarrassed for myself. I didn't want that.

Forget, Surrender, Deny, Repeat

So I buried my feelings. At times those stuffed-down feelings would resurface and I would ask God for a husband. I'd journal about it, pray fervently, and be on the lookout for who God might bring. Then I would try to forget about my longings, surrender them to God, and convince myself I didn't want to be married, anyway. I told myself, and other people, that it wasn't important. That I was completely content. That I had come to terms with where I was.

That was a lie. A lie I wanted to believe because it seemed that everyone who loved God was satisfied with their circumstances. Besides, it seemed better to deny a longing that might never be fulfilled than it would be to keep longing. It certainly was less painful. Others had accepted their unfulfilled longings. They had come to terms with their singleness or infertility or discouraging careers.

When they finally let go of their desires, they gained a sense of stability. So I was torn about what to do. I begged God to take away this desire, but he didn't. So I cried out to him to meet me in the midst of this unfulfilled longing.

For years he met me there. And then God blessed me with a husband who is beyond my expectations.

Fulfilled, Yet Yearning

And yet in other things—with longings just as real and intense—God has not given me what I was yearning for. He has left me with unmet desires. Desires that may not be fulfilled this side of heaven. Desires that I may live with forever. Right now I want a healthy body that can do the things I want to do. With post-polio syndrome, I am deteriorating daily, much more rapidly than I am prepared for. Some days I wake up with intense pain that gives way to a dull ache that drags on throughout the day. On those days, my arms are limited to basic tasks like eating and dressing. If I can use them at all.

It's been excruciating. I have sobbed and questioned God, begging for deliverance. For me, as a "helper" personality type, serving has been one of my greatest joys. And when that role is reversed and I am the one who needs to be served, I feel uneasy. Uncomfortable. A burden. I want to be the perfect wife who makes great meals, keeps a neat house, and has boundless energy. A thoughtful mother who serves her children tirelessly. A dependable friend whom others can count on for anything. But I often can't be any of those things. Rather than serving, I have to be served. At the most inconvenient times.

Friends have encouraged me to relax and be content with my circumstances. To give up my longing for things to be different. They say that is the only way to have peace. I wish I could. I have known for over a decade that my body is failing, yet it is still hard not to meet the physical needs of others. I am wired to serve. So whenever I can't do that and the roles are reversed, I grieve.

These limitations bother me daily. And whenever they do, I am invited to surrender them to God. As an act of worship. A living sacrifice. An offering of faith and trust in God. The Bible says that there is great gain in godliness with contentment (1 Tim. 6:6). God has a reason for all of our circumstances. We should live life to the fullest with what we've been given. We should learn to see his grace and find joy wherever we are.

At the same time, it's unhealthy to deny our pain and pretend everything is fine when it isn't. It's okay to want things to be different. It's dangerous to squelch our longings, stuffing them down so deep that we are devoid of emotions and passion.

Honesty Is Better

It's far better to be completely honest with God. To offer my longings up to him. To ask him to change the situation or give me the grace to handle it. Strangely enough, that process of crying out to God and being honest about my pain has drawn me close to Jesus.

False contentment doesn't do that. Quite the opposite, feigned contentment pulls me away from Christ because I can't even see my need for him. Deadening our desires may make us stoics, but it won't make us passionate followers of Christ. Contentment that is borne out of suppressing our longings leads to empty platitudes at best and bitter hypocrisy at worst.

We all have longings. Crying out to God to fulfill them or change them or give us the strength to endure them strengthens our faith. Denying our longings under the guise of contentment may keep us from pain, may look more spiritual, and may make us less emotional, but it can lead to spiritual deadness.

God may change my desires and bring lasting contentment even when he denies my cherished requests. That would be a great gift. But it does not always happen that way. And if it doesn't—if I still feel those raw places in my soul, if I still long for something more—he may want me to lean into him more closely, trust him more fervently, and cling to him more tightly. And that is a mercy as well.

Life is full of pain. Sometimes God miraculously delivers us. When he does, we rejoice and give him glory. He makes all things new and brings beauty from ashes. Sometimes we aren't delivered, but he gives us true contentment in our circumstances, so the world can see his peace and satisfaction. And sometimes he leaves us with a constant ache, a reminder that this world is not our home, and we are just strangers passing through.

This relentless ache is what drives me to my knees, brings me to Jesus, makes me long for heaven. And perhaps in heaven, I will thank God most for my unfulfilled longings because they did the deepest, most lasting work in my soul.

But I am afflicted and in pain; let your salvation, O God, set me on high! (Psalm 69:29)

DEPENDENCE

Self-sufficiency and independence are part of the American way. Most of us have embraced these ideals. They allow us to provide for ourselves with relatively little uncertainty or inconvenience.

We're all prone to viewing our Maker as a good back-up plan. We work to craft and control our future without outside assistance, knowing God is always there if things go awry.

Goodbye Autonomy, Hello Dependence

I was operating quite well on that principle until about 15 years ago, when a diagnosis of post-polio syndrome abruptly ended my romance with autonomy. Since then my life has been characterized by dependence: dependence on friends, dependence on family, dependence on God.

Each year I'm able to do less for myself. Each year I must rely on others more. With post-polio, my muscles will eventually stop working; they cannot be rejuvenated. They are slowly dying. Since I have no idea how much strength I have left, I must trust God to provide the energy I need each day.

My condition is both frustrating and frightening. It's hard to decide where to direct my waning energy, to figure

out what good things I must say no to because they're too
physically costly.

Praying for Just Enough

As a result, several friends started praying that my
strength would be like the widow of Zarephath's oil and
flour. That there would always be enough. That I would
never lack. That my energy would never run out.

We read the story of the widow of Zarephath in 1
Kings 17. Each day she was given just enough oil and flour
for her needs, but no more. And she never *knew* if she'd
have what she needed for the next day. She simply knew
that if the Lord didn't provide for her each day, she and
her son would starve. She had no resources of her own, no
cushion to fall back on, no way to see the future. But this
widow had God. And he was enough.

Her story is a beautiful picture of utter dependence
on God. It's a beautiful example of how God provides for
us. A beautiful illustration of trusting him for our daily
needs. Beautiful, that is, for other people. I love watching
God work in others' lives that way. It inspires me. But I
don't want such absolute dependence myself. I wouldn't
willingly choose to be like the widow of Zarephath.

But I Want a Full Flask

I don't like living with scarcity. I don't like having just
enough to meet my needs. I don't like being dependent. It
makes me feel vulnerable. In my economy, I want a full oil
flask and overflowing flour jar. I want to see exactly how

and when God will provide for my needs. I want a guarantee I can independently verify.

That's because, deep down, I'd rather depend on myself than on God. Though I want to serve him with my whole heart, trusting him in the dark can be frightening; it's far easier when the future looks bright. I'd rather praise God for his abundant provision than daily depend on him to meet my basic needs.

Thankfully, he doesn't give me what I want or what I would choose on my own. He has something more magnificent in mind. He knows that my security and confidence are best rooted in him, not in the good things he gives. Even though his gifts may be wonderful blessings, they cannot be my source of hope.

It's wise to save money so we have enough to retire. But facing retirement with little savings may force us to depend on God in ways a large bank account never would. It's wonderful to have great health and boundless energy. But being ill and relying on others for assistance may drive us to our knees, quicker and longer, each day. It's a joy to have a house full of loving, obedient children. But crying out to God because of infertility or wayward kids may draw us into a deeper relationship with him.

Better to Have a Trouble

"There is no greater mercy that I know of on earth than good health except it be sickness; and that has often been a greater mercy to me than health," Charles Spurgeon said. "It is a good thing to be without a trouble; but it is a better thing to have a trouble, and know how to get grace enough to bear it."[15]

It is a better thing to have a trouble, and know how to get grace enough to bear it. That's because dependence is always better than self-sufficiency in the kingdom of God. Self-sufficiency leads to pride and selfishness, while dependence leads to humility and intimacy with the Lord. Dependence yields good fruit in our lives. As Spurgeon apparently said elsewhere: "I have learned to kiss the wave that throws me against the Rock of Ages."[16]

Anything that makes me dependent on God is a good thing, perhaps the best thing. This is, of course, profoundly biblical. The children of Israel were given manna every day. They couldn't provide for themselves; they had to depend on their all-providing God. Jesus underscored the importance of day-by-day dependence when he taught us to pray, saying, "Give us this day our daily bread" (Matt. 6:11). God alone provides all we need each day, even our very breath. Any sense of independence from him, then, is an illusion.

Dashed Against the Rock of Ages

Because of my sinfulness, I still wouldn't choose to be like the widow of Zarephath. I wouldn't choose dependence over independence. I wouldn't choose scarcity over abundance. But as God has chosen them for me, I have found them all to be streams of unspeakable blessing.

I am thankful the Lord continues to give me what is best for me, not what I would choose for myself. I am consumed with my own comfort; he is consumed with my eternal joy. My places of famine and desolation have become the places where I see him most clearly. Not only does he meet my every need; he wondrously fills me with himself.

And, miraculously, I am learning to be grateful for every wave that dashes me against the Rock of Ages.

WHY DOESN'T GOD HEAL EVERYONE?

As I read the words from my old journal, I vividly recall my emotions. Shame, humiliation, doubt. The entry is dated April 16, 1983. I was in my second semester of college.

Faith, Healing, and Faith Healing

I remember the day well. My friends suggested I go to the meeting, but I was resistant. I had been to healing services before. Each time I had expected a miraculous healing. Each time I believed it would happen. Each time I had returned disappointed. I wanted to shield myself from further frustration, but at the same time, I so wanted to be healed. All day I felt unsettled, vacillating between fear and excitement.

Though we arrived early, the room was packed. The only seats left were in the first row. As we walked to the front of the auditorium, I was painfully aware of my limp. Everyone knew I had come for healing. My presence seemed to intensify the excitement. I could tell everyone was wondering if they were going to witness a verifiable miracle.

After a short sermon, people started lining up. This travelling evangelist touched people where they were hurting and prayed for them, commanding them to be healed in the name of Jesus. And all of them were healed. Hip pains, ear aches, migraines—all disappeared immediately. My stomach was in knots when someone grabbed my hand and led me onto the stage. There was silence as everyone turned to me. I was terrified.

I sat in a chair while this man pulled on my legs and told me that one leg was longer than the other. He fixed that. Then he touched my shoulders and legs, claimed my healing, and asked me to walk. When I did, nothing was different. He prayed again. Still, no change. He was irritated. Maybe a bit embarrassed. He looked at me and said, "I've done all I can do. The rest is up to you."

He walked away and declared with a dismissive wave, "I see that you do not have the faith to be healed. You need to go home and pray and ask God to give you more faith. I'm going to do another healing service and baptism tomorrow. If you have the faith, come to that meeting and you will be healed." He turned his attention to the next person in line while my friends helped me off the stage.

I was mortified. No one had ever said it was my fault before. No one had questioned my faith in the process. No one had blamed me for my disability. I sat there, humiliated, trying to figure out the next step. I was simultaneously embarrassed, insecure, and irate.

Aftermath

Late that night I penned my journal entry. I began with, "I'm so confused and I don't know what to think . . . if you want me to be healed Lord, give me the faith." Doubts started to overwhelm me. I felt desperate. The following day I wrote, "I have so little faith . . . you say if we lack faith we must but ask. Lord, I want to be healed . . . help me to trust that I will be."

Over the next few days, my emotions were on a roller coaster, alternating between begging God for the faith to be healed and demonizing this man who had humiliated me. I then decided that he was wrong. He was a false teacher. My faith was strong, and no one could question it.

I needed grace. Grace for myself, to see that my healing didn't rest on me. Grace for this man, who was attempting to walk out his gifting. Grace for my friends, who were trying to help me discern truth. When I was criticized, I assumed that no fault lay with me. It was totally this man's mistake. No one should have questioned my faith. But as I looked at my heart and what lay at the root of my anger, I saw my own sins of self-righteousness, pride, and arrogance.

But at the same time, I don't believe faith healers can heal whomever they wish. They can only heal those whom God has chosen to restore. The glorious message of the gospel is that God's plan and promises are not dependent on us. They are wholly dependent on him, for he has done it all. God alone decides for whom and when and where healing will occur.

Thorns Remaining and Thorns Removed

Personally, I would love to be physically healed. Or at least for my post-polio deterioration to stop. It would make my days a lot easier. But God in his wisdom has chosen not to remove this thorn. I don't understand when or why God chooses to heal. It remains a mystery. I wish I knew why devout faithful Christians die young of cancer and other not-so-faithful people receive inexplicable healing, when the former are seeking God daily and the latter utter a one-time quick prayer. It doesn't seem fair.

Yet I have received miraculous physical healing myself. When I was eight years old, I used ankle braces. The doctors said I couldn't walk without them. But God changed that in an instant through a faith healer who felt called to come to our home and pray over me. I haven't worn braces since, and *the doctors to this day are astounded*. It doesn't make medical sense.

So why didn't God go all the way and heal me completely? Why did he just stop with getting rid of my braces? Why didn't he do the more astonishing miracle? I don't know for certain. But I do know that God has done a deeper healing in my life because of my disability. He has taught me to trust him in the dark. He has refined my character through loss. And he has given me an incredible joy in him. Those things are more valuable to me than physical healing.

God's power is being made perfect in my weakness. Paradoxically, it is often in the not being healed, the crying out to God, the trusting him when it hurts that I see God most clearly. A Puritan prayer from *The Valley of Vision*, puts it this way: "Lord, in the daytime, stars can be seen from deepest wells, and the deeper the wells, the brighter thy stars shine."

While I'd like to understand God's mysteries, I don't feel I need to. My finite mind cannot comprehend the infinite. But I am certain that God is purposeful. I'm positive life isn't random and God isn't capricious. And whether I am physically healed or not, I can rest on God's unchanging grace.

That prayer from *The Valley of Vision* ends with this: "Let me find thy light in my darkness, thy life in my death, thy joy in my sorrow, thy grace in my sin, thy riches in my poverty, thy glory in my valley."[17]

For in Christ, I have indeed found his light in my darkness and his joy in my sorrow.

WHEELCHAIRS AND WORSHIP

Joni's earrings catch my attention.

They are hammered gold with crinkled edges that flash brilliant. I am captivated. I've heard about these earrings. They were once smooth and square, polished and perfect. She treasured them—an unexpected gift from a friend. But she inadvertently dropped one on her office floor, crushing it under her wheelchair tire, the crunching sound betraying the damage.

A jeweler told her he couldn't fix it. But he could make the smooth one match the other. It was a risk, but she decided to trust him. In the back room she heard hammering and grinding. Did he know what he was doing? But he returned with a matching second earring. Marred and mangled. But strangely magnificent.

Battered Beautiful

I stare at these earrings. They are exquisite. From my vantage, they are not marred at all. Quite the opposite, they look like the work of a skilled craftsman. The damage has produced something breathtaking.

The lesson is vivid. I don't want to struggle, to take the hard road, to be bruised. I'd prefer an easy, smooth life.

But it is the pounding that produces character, character that reflects light. As I see the twisted gold shimmering, I am amazed at the beauty from what has been battered.

As we talk, my gaze shifts from Joni's earrings to her hands. We're having dinner and I'm watching her eat. This is not idle curiosity; I know with post-polio that my arms are failing and I, too, may struggle to feed myself. She frequently needs help and must be content with the way others help her. How they cut her food, what they put on her plate, when they can attend to her needs.

As a foodie, I cannot imagine eating that way. I want each bite to be exactly the way I envision it. I watch and wonder if I could accept help with such grace. After a moment of observing, I know that I could not. At least not in my own strength. I say to her quietly, "Joni, this must be so hard—you can't always have things the way you want them." I'm voicing my own struggles, my own fears, my own pain.

She laughs and says, "I'm a type A person, and with quadriplegia, nothing is exactly the way I want it. Nothing but my writing." She leans towards me, looks me straight in the eye and declares with unwavering certainty, "But all these little decisions, these everyday things I surrender, the choices I make daily will one day shine in glory. They will all count."

Everything Counts

I swallow hard. I needed to hear that. These little choices, these seemingly insignificant ways that I have to relinquish what I want, when no one sees and no one else knows, they all count. Because Someone does see, and Someone does know. Not one of these sacrifices will be forgotten. One day, they will all shine in glory. They will all count.

I think about her moment-by-moment surrenderings. Her choices to be grateful when things are not perfect. Her dying to self. These are acts of worship. They have eternal significance. I realize that all my responses matter as well. I can show the surpassing worth of Christ when I suffer well, when I joyfully accept circumstances that are less than perfect, when I lay down my need to control. Giving up my right to have something exactly as I want can be an act of worship.

Joni Eareckson Tada has mentored me from afar as I have learned, through her writing, how to press on in the midst of suffering. She has displayed what it looks like to be abandoned to God. She has shown me that the glory of God is worth suffering for, living for, and dying for. As I have watched her, I have silently affirmed, "If this is what affliction does in someone's life, if this is the way it could draw me to God, if this is the way it could demonstrate Jesus to a watching world, sign me up for suffering."

Joni shows me that God is valuable not because he makes our lives easier. He is valuable because he is the Lord of the universe and knowing him is better than anything in this life. Knowing him is the ultimate joy. Knowing him is worth any ordeal we may endure.

This is a God worthy of worship. The God who took a woman who wanted to die after being rendered a quadriplegic and so changed her from the inside out that she could later say, "I am grateful for my quadriplegia."[18]

Joni's book, *When God Weeps*, was life-changing for me and helped forge my theology. Some of my favorite quotes are:

Nothing happens by accident. . . . Not even tragedy. . . . Not even sins committed against us.

Every sorrow we taste will one day prove to be the best possible thing that could've happened. We will thank God endlessly in heaven for the trials he sent us here.

God permits what he hates to achieve what he loves.

Either God rules, or Satan sets the world's agenda and God is limited to reacting. In which case, the Almighty would become Satan's cleanup boy, sweeping up after the devil has trampled through and done his worst, finding a way to wring good out of the situation somehow. But it wasn't his best plan for you, wasn't plan A, wasn't exactly what he had in mind. In other words, although God would manage to patch things up, your suffering itself would be meaningless.

Colossians 1:24 says "now I rejoice in what was suffered for you, and I fill up in my flesh what is lacking in regard to Christ's afflictions, for the sake of his body, which is the church." Nothing is lacking when it comes to what Christ did on the cross. It is finished, just as he said. But something is lacking when it comes to showcasing the salvation story to others. Jesus isn't around in the flesh, but you and I are. When we suffer and handle it with grace, we're like walking billboards advertising the positive way God works in the life of someone who suffers.

The greatest good suffering can do for me is to increase my capacity for God.[19]

Joni closes her inspiring memoir, *The God I Love,* saying, "There are more important things in life than walking."[20] And after knowing Joni, I have to agree.

WHEN THE PAIN
NEVER ENDS

I like sunny days. Days with little drama, minimal stress, no pain. When there's nothing to worry about and life is laid-back and easy. Like sipping lemonade on my back porch with a cool summer breeze in the air.

But as I look back over my life, those simple, light-hearted days are not the ones for which I'm most grateful. I'm most grateful for the days when I've had to fight for faith. The days I've called out to God in desperation and pain. The days I have barely survived, struggled to make it through, wondered if life was worth it, after all. The days that have driven me to my knees. These have molded my character, grown my dependence, and made me see Jesus. For me, gratitude for those days is often in retrospect. Looking back, I can rejoice at what God wrought through my trials. When the pain is gone and only the fruit remains, I see the value of my suffering.

Wearing Trials

But for some trials, the pain never passes. These are the long-term, ongoing, daily struggles that grind away at us. Chronic illness. A difficult marriage. A child who is "atypical." A disappointing career. Financial worries. Depression.

Unfulfilled longings. When we live with these wearing trials, we tend to fantasize about how pleasant and normal our lives would be without them. I've frequently thought, "If I just didn't have to struggle with this one problem, I could handle everything else. This problem dwarfs all the others and makes my life more challenging than the lives of people around me."

What I don't see is that this one overarching problem is what is drawing me closest to Jesus. I have learned from saints, living and dead, that I need to thank God for my deepest suffering. Believers who have thanked God for blindness, for prison, and for quadriplegia. Unthinkable suffering, which most would consider unbearable, these Christ-followers have seen as God's gifts.

Gifts wrapped in black, but gifts nonetheless.

What Sunny Days Can't Do

These heroes—specifically George Matheson, Alexander Solzhenitsyn, and Joni Eareckson Tada—have mentored me from afar, teaching me the value of my thorns. Rather than summarizing their thoughts, I want to let their own words stand, as they each describe what God has done through their trials.

The first, George Matheson, was a well-known blind Scottish preacher who wrote the hymn, "O Love That Will Not Let Me Go." He says of his blindness:

> My God, I have never thanked Thee for my
> thorn. I have thanked Thee a thousand times
> for my roses, but not once for my thorn. I have
> been looking forward to a world where I shall

get compensation for my cross; but I have never thought of my cross as itself a present glory.

Teach me the glory of my cross; teach me the value of my thorn. Show me that I have climbed to Thee by the path of pain. Show me that my tears have made my rainbows.[21]

The second, Alexander Solzhenitsyn, was a Russian writer who endured prison and forced-labor camps under Joseph Stalin. It was there he became a Christian, and went on to write:

> It was granted to me to carry away from my prison years on my bent back, which nearly broke beneath its load, this essential experience: how a human being becomes evil and how good. In the intoxication of youthful successes I had felt myself to be infallible, and I was therefore cruel. In the surfeit of power I was a murderer and an oppressor. In my most evil moments I was convinced that I was doing good, and I was well supplied with systematic arguments. It was only when I lay there on rotting prison straw that I sensed within myself the first stirrings of good. Gradually it was disclosed to me that the line separating good and evil passes not through states, nor between classes, nor between political parties either—but right through every human heart—and through all human hearts. . . . That is why I turn back to the years of my imprisonment and say, sometimes to the astonishment of those about me: "Bless you, prison!" I . . . have served

enough time there. I nourished my soul there, and I say without hesitation: "Bless you, prison, for having been in my life!"[22]

The third, Joni Eareckson Tada, is a Christian author, speaker, and ministry leader who became a quadriplegic at age 17 after a diving accident. Joni says:

Most of us are able to thank God for his grace, comfort, and sustaining power in a trial, but we don't thank him *for* the problem, just finding him in it.

But many decades in a wheelchair have taught me to not segregate my Savior from the suffering he allows, as though a broken neck—or in your case, a broken ankle, heart or home— merely "happens" and then God shows up after the fact to wrestle something good out of it. No, the God of the Bible is bigger than that. Much bigger.

And so is the capacity of your soul. Maybe this wheelchair felt like a horrible tragedy in the beginning, but I give God thanks *in* my wheelchair. . . . I'm grateful *for* my quadriplegia. It's a bruising of a blessing. A gift wrapped in black. It's the shadowy companion that walks with me daily, pulling and pushing me into the arms of my Saviour. And *that's* where the joy is.

. . .

Your "wheelchair", whatever it is, falls well within the overarching decrees of God. Your hardship and heartache come from his wise and

kind hand and for that, you can be grateful. In it
and for it.[23]

I thank God for these fellow believers, who have shown
me how precious my pain is. In the hands of an almighty
God, my tears have made my rainbows, shown me my own
depravity, and pushed me to the arms of my tender Savior.

And all of those blessings far outweigh the fleeting
happiness of sipping lemonade on sunny days.

I am in despair. I looked for pity, but there was none, and for comforters, but I found none.
(Psalm 69:20)

WHAT IF THE WORST HAPPENS?

I found myself growing fearful. Not a heart-stopping, all-encompassing fear, but the kind of constant gnawing that creeps into your bones when you hear bad news or see something going awry. When you extrapolate the discouraging trends of the present into the future and assume things will never change. When you think about where you're headed and feel your stomach tighten.

Questions lingered in the back of my mind. What if I continue on this path? What if nothing ever gets better? What if the worst happens?

What If?

I've spent a lifetime considering the what-ifs. Those questions have a way of making me uneasy, destroying my peace, leaving me feeling hopeless. When negative possibilities loom before me, I can't seem to rein in my thoughts. Just asking "What if . . ." unsettles me.

People in the Bible were unsettled by what-if questions, too. When he was told to lead the Israelites, Moses asked God, "What if they don't believe me?" Abraham's servant asked about Isaac's future wife, "What if the young woman refuses to come with me?" Joseph's brothers asked,

"What if Joseph bears a grudge against us?" All of them wondered what would happen if circumstances went awry. Just like we do.

We all face a staggering array of what-ifs. Some are minor inconveniences while others have potentially life-altering repercussions. What if I lose my job? What if I never have children? What if I get cancer? What if my spouse dies? What if my husband never loves me? What if my child never believes in Jesus?

The uncomfortable truth is any of those things could happen. No one is free from tragedy or pain. There are no guarantees of an easy life. For any of us. Ever.

I was considering this sobering reality on a silent retreat years ago. Over the course of several days, I had brought numerous longings and requests before the Lord. I wanted them fulfilled. When would God do it? As I penned my thoughts, I felt that familiar fear gripping me.

Enough?

The question echoed in my mind: What if my inmost longings are never met and my nightmares come true? I didn't even want to entertain that possibility. As I sat in the empty chapel poring over my Bible, I sensed God asking the same question I have wrestled with for decades. "Am I enough? Even if those frightening things happen, am I sufficient?" Each time that question had come up in the past, I'd pushed it out of my mind.

But in the stillness of the chapel, I knew I needed to face this. I sensed God whispering again, "Vaneetha, am I enough? If none of your dreams come true, am I enough? If your health spirals downward and you end up in an institution, am I enough? If your children rebel and never walk closely with me, am I enough? If you never remarry and never feel loved by a man again, am I enough? If your ministry doesn't flourish and you never see fruit from it, am I enough? If your suffering continues and you never see purpose in it, am I enough?"

I wish I could have automatically responded, "Yes Lord, you are enough." But I agonized. The weight of those questions felt crushing. I didn't want to give up my dreams, surrender those things that were dear to me, relinquish what I felt entitled to. I reflected on my unwritten, one-way "contract" with God, where I promise to do my part if he fulfills my longings. I reluctantly admitted that part of my desire to be faithful was rooted in my expectation of a payback. Didn't God owe me something? But what if I didn't get it?

I knew I needed to relinquish my desires, but I was incapable of doing it myself. I begged God for help. To release my expectations. To let go of my dreams and embrace his. To not predicate my obedience on his gifts. I sobbed as I opened my hands, filled with my dreams, and surrendered them to him. I didn't want to love God for what he could do for me. I wanted to love God for who he is. To worship him because he is worthy and not because I expected something in return.

Even If

God's presence overwhelmed me as I knelt in the semi-darkness and relinquished my expectations. He reminded me that I have something far better than a reassurance that my dreaded what-ifs won't happen. I have the assurance that *even if* they do happen, God will be there in the midst of them. He will carry me. He will comfort me. He will tenderly care for me. God doesn't promise me a trouble-free life. But he does promise that he will be there in the midst of my sorrows.

In the Bible, Shadrach, Meshach, and Abednego were not guaranteed deliverance. Just before Nebuchadnezzar delivered them to the fire, they offered some of the most courageous words ever spoken. "If we are thrown into the blazing furnace, the God we serve is able to deliver us from it. . . . But *even if* he does not, we want you to know . . . that we will not serve your gods" (Dan. 3:17–18 NIV).

Even if the worst happens, God's grace is sufficient. Those three young men faced the fire without fear because they knew that no matter the outcome, it would ultimately be for their good and God's glory. They did not ask *what if* the worst happened. They were satisfied knowing that *even if* the worst happened, God would take care of them.

Even if. Those two simple words can take the fear out of life. *Replacing "what if" with "even if" in our mental vocabulary is one of the most liberating exchanges we can ever make. We trade our irrational fears of an uncertain future for the loving assurance of an unchanging God.* We see that *even if* the very worst happens, God will carry us. He will still be good. And he will never leave us.

At the end of Habakkuk, we see another beautiful picture of even-if. Habakkuk wants deliverance for his people and pleads with God to save them. But he closes his book with an exquisite even-if.

> Even if the fig tree does not bloom and the vines have no grapes,

even if the olive tree fails to produce
and the fields yield no food,
even if the sheep pen is empty
and the stalls have no cattle—
even then,
I will be happy with the Lord.
I will truly find joy in God, who saves me.
(Hab. 3:17–18 GW)

THE LONELINESS
OF SUFFERING

One of the hardest things for me about suffering is loneliness.

Inevitably I feel isolated. Though my friends can help, they cannot share my sorrow. It is too deep a well. When loss is fresh, people are all around. They call, offer help, send cards, and bring meals. Their care helps ease the razor-sharp pain. For a while.

But then they stop. There are no more meals. The phone is strangely silent. And the mailbox is empty. No one knows what to say. They aren't sure what to ask. So mostly they say nothing.

Sometimes that's fine. It's hard to talk about pain. And I never want pity, with the mournful look, the squeeze on the arm, and the hushed question, "So how are you?" I don't know how to answer that; I don't know how I am. Part of me is crushed. I will never be the same again. My life is radically altered. But another part of me craves normalcy. A return to the familiar. To blend into the crowd.

I Don't Know What I Want

I want to be grateful for my friends' support. And on the best of days, I can see and appreciate all of their efforts.

But on the worst of days, I feel frustrated and angry. I wonder why people aren't meeting my needs. Don't they know what I want? Can't they read the signs? Why can't they figure out what would make me feel better?

They can't figure it out because I don't know myself. This is the crazy part of grief for me. I don't know what I want. I have no idea what will satisfy me. And somehow, no matter what others do, they cannot meet my expectations. Expectations that are fickle. And one-sided. And reflect my self-absorption.

Intense pain, physical or emotional, has a way of narrowing my world. I become fixated on myself—my needs, my pain, my life. Somehow I forget that other people have their own pain and their own lives. They want to help, but they can only do so much.

Alone with God

While I am frustrated that others aren't easing my pain, I need to remember that there is a part of suffering that I must bear myself. Paul addresses that very tension. In Galatians 6:2, he says, "Bear one another's burdens, and so fulfill the law of Christ." And then, three verses later, he reminds them, "For each will have to bear his own load" (Gal. 6:5).

The word Paul uses for *burden* implies burdens that exceed our strength. In Paul's day, travelers often had heavy loads to transport. Others would relieve them by carrying their burdens for a while. Without help, those loads could be crushing. This could be likened to the tangible help we can offer others—our acts of service, our continual prayers, our physical presence.

His word for *load* is something proportioned to our individual strength. It could be a pack carried by a marching soldier. That could be the ongoing work of processing our grief. The parts of our suffering that no one else can carry for us. The burdens we must shoulder ourselves.

Even the closest, most caring friends cannot be with us in our deepest pain. They may weep with us, but they cannot walk with us all the way.

Jesus understands that. In his moments of greatest need, his friends deserted him. Friends who said they would die for him could not even stay awake and pray with him.

So in the garden, Jesus found himself alone. With God. Just like we are. In the end, we are all left alone with God.

Where Do I Go?

So what do we do when we feel drained and empty? When no one understands our suffering and no one seems to care? When we feel discouraged and tired and unbearably lonely?

Read the Bible and pray. Read the Bible even when it feels like eating cardboard. And pray even when it feels like talking to a wall.

Does it sound simple? It is. Does it also sound exceedingly hard? It is that as well. But reading the Bible and praying is the only way I have ever found out of my grief.

There are no shortcuts to healing. Often I wish there were, because I'd like to move on from the pain. But in many ways, I am thankful for the transformative process I undergo. A process requiring that I read the Bible and pray.

Not Just Reading

When I say read, I don't mean just reading words for a specific amount of time. I mean meditating on them. Writing down what God is saying to me. Asking God to reveal himself to me. Believing God uses Scripture to teach and to comfort me. To teach me wonderful things in his law (Ps. 119:18). To comfort me with his promises (Ps. 119:76).

Reading this way changes cardboard into manna. I echo Jeremiah who said, "Your words were found, and I ate them, and your words became to me a joy and the delight of my heart" (Jer. 15:16).

Not Just Praying

And when I say pray, I don't mean a rote recitation of requests and mindless words. I mean really praying. Speaking to God as honestly as I would speak to a friend. Praying through a psalm. Desperately crying out to him. Asking him for specific help. Expecting him to answer.

What transforms me is spending time with Jesus, sitting with him, lamenting to him, talking to him, and listening to him. As much as I would like friends to comfort me, no one has ever met me the way God has. No one's words have ever changed me the way Scripture has. And no one's presence has ever encouraged me the way the Holy Spirit has. My friends may help me, but they cannot heal me. It is only the living God, and his living word, who can do that.

This path of suffering, of heartache, of loneliness takes me directly to my Savior. Which is the only path worth taking. For only Jesus can heal me.

THE COMFORT
OF OTHERS

When pain overwhelms me, I long for companionship.

I want someone to talk to me, weep with me, sit with me. I want someone to put human flesh on God's comfort. That may sound unspiritual to some people. It always sounded faintly unspiritual to me. It seemed weak to want comfort from other people. I thought that if God alone were sufficient to meet my every need, I should never want anyone else.

And of course, he is sufficient. We need the presence of God more than we need anything else. He is the God of all comfort. His fellowship and love are what our hearts need most.

The Gift of Community

Yet at the same time, I also long for the comfort of my friends. I need community. And I need it most acutely when I am suffering. This need has always felt somehow unholy. A part of my sinful flesh that would one day be redeemed. A weakness that would diminish over time. I assumed my role in community should be just to serve, not to receive.

Then I saw it. When I first noticed it, it startled me. In his darkest moments, Jesus wanted his friends. Mark 14:32–34 says:

> And they went to a place called Gethsemane. And he said to his disciples, "Sit here while I pray." And he took with him Peter and James and John, and began to be greatly distressed and troubled. And he said to them, "My soul is very sorrowful, even to death. Remain here and watch."

Jesus didn't want to be alone in his suffering. He wanted human companionship. Jesus didn't ask his disciples to accompany him when he was communing with his Father. He often arose early in the morning to be with God by himself. But we see that in his hour of desperation, when he was facing unspeakable agony, he asked his friends to be with him.

Simply Human

Since God the Father has always had unbroken fellowship in the Trinity, he has never lacked community. But Jesus in the garden knew that his fellowship with God would soon be completely severed, and he longed for companionship. Clearly this longing was not sinfully weak or needy. It did not reflect a lack of trust in God or a fragile faith. It was simply human. God incarnate longed for fellowship. Because God created us to live in community.

In the same way, our friends often long for presence in their suffering. Caring for them from a distance is not enough. They aren't looking for answers to their deepest questions or solutions to their most pressing problems. They just need our presence.

For some of us, that's a difficult task. Much harder than it sounds. It's easier to tell stories. Offer advice. Lecture about optimism. Recite a Bible verse or even deliver a mini-sermon. Those are easier than just being with someone in their grief. We want instant relief, for ourselves and for our friends. So it's tempting to try to rush their healing, fix their problems, alleviate their doubts. Then we feel we've accomplished something.

Simply Sitting

Sitting seems so useless. So inefficient. So pointless. And yet it is amazingly valuable. Our presence alone is a gift. As we sit, our suffering friends may not respond to conversation. Some communicate little in their grief. They process internally. They offer no words. Maybe a few tears. Maybe a vacant look. Maybe just a chasm of emptiness.

Other people are verbal processors, flooding us with words about how they are feeling and what they are thinking. Most of these words are not carefully thought out. Or wholly theological. They are at best painful groans not intended for evaluation or judgment.

But no matter how they process, no one is asking us for a deluge of words in response. They just want someone to be there with them.

Simply being present with our friends has more of a healing effect than we can imagine. I still remember a friend who often stopped by the house after our son, Paul, died. She rarely spoke and mostly sat with me unobtrusively. I loved having her there. I didn't feel that I had to make any conversation. But at the same time I knew she would listen if I wanted to talk. I didn't want to be alone, though I would never have verbalized it that way. I simply knew that her presence was a great comfort.

Author Joe Bayly had a similar experience after burying his second son. Bayly says:

> I was sitting, torn by grief. Someone came and talked to me of God's dealings, of why it happened, of hope beyond the grave. He talked constantly, he said things I knew were true. I was unmoved, except to wish he'd go away. He finally did.
>
> Another came and sat beside me. He didn't talk. He didn't ask leading questions. He just sat beside me for an hour or more, listened when I said something, answered briefly, prayed simply, left.
>
> I was moved. I was comforted. I hated to see him go.[24]

I understand Bayly's first friend. He wanted to make things better. He wanted to do something, and words seemed to be the answer. He thought his words would bring comfort.

I am well familiar with that attitude. When there is something to be *done*, I want to do it. But when there is nothing else to do, I often flee. It's less uncomfortable. Less uncomfortable for me, that is.

Neonatal pediatrician Dr. John Wyatt does not flee. In his practice, he has had to make difficult and painful clinical decisions. Sometimes there are no treatments left for his tiny patients; his training and expertise can do no more. It is then that Wyatt simply sits and weeps with the grieving parents. And perhaps that is his greatest service. He says in his book, *Matters of Life and Death*,

> Suffering in another human being is a call to the rest of us to stand in community. It is a call to be there. Suffering is not a question which demands an answer, it is not a problem which requires a solution, it is a mystery which demands a presence.[25]

What a powerful reminder of how we can comfort those who suffer. And how others can comfort us as well. For suffering is a mystery that demands a presence.

WHEN YOU STRUGGLE TO BELIEVE GOD LOVES YOU

"I struggle to believe that God loves me."

A dear friend emailed that to me months ago, and I've carried it around in my heart ever since. I understand what she means. Those feelings have bombarded me countless times. Often on days when despair overwhelms me. Days that begin by struggling to get out of bed, wondering why I should even go on. Days that are fueled only by duty, which is an excruciating way to live.

Those are the days on which I have wondered: *Is there more to life than this? How can I believe God loves me when I'm existing at best and feeling shattered at worst?* I would look at my friends' lives and feel cheated. I knew they had their own struggles, but from my perspective, God streamed sunshine over their days while mine were overshadowed by clouds and pouring rain. It was hard to see God's love in that.

Rain for a Reason

And rain in my life usually came when I least expected it. When it was the most inconvenient. When it was the most painful. The rain seemed to have no purpose but to bring upheaval and pain. I struggled to see any good in it.

Because in the midst of being shaped, it's hard to see anything. When I am being pelted by driving rain, everything is clouded and gray. My vision is obscured. All I can think about is finding peace. Being dry. Basking in the sunshine. And wondering if I'll ever get there.

But after the rain has passed, or even when it takes a break, I can look around and see what God has produced through the slashing storm. A dependence on God that is unmistakable. A faith that has been tested. A trust that is unaffected by circumstances. When God shakes what can be shaken, what remains is lasting (Heb. 12:27). And that is a gift beyond all compare.

As Joel 2:23 reads in one translation, "Rejoice in the Lord your God! For the rain he sends demonstrates his faithfulness"(NLT).

When I get a glimpse of God's perspective, I see my trials very differently. I see what they are producing in me, the ways they are shaping me, and how they bring glory to God. I can be grateful for what God teaches me about himself through the storm. My faith is often strengthened, my love for God is deepened, and my worldly attachments seem less enticing. And then I can thank God for the storm. I can see that it was brought to me out of extravagant love. I can see that the rain God sends does indeed demonstrate his faithfulness.

Rain That Reframes

The Bible shows me that rain is a gift from God. Rain yields fruit in our lives. With all sunshine and no rain, we become brittle and dried-up—useful for no one and nothing. Abundant, life-giving fruit requires rain. D. A. Carson says, "One of the things held out to grieving or suffering believers is the prospect of being more fruitful than they could have ever imagined."[26]

So in the pouring rain, when our trials are fiercest, God is demonstrating his love for us most powerfully. When we don't even feel his presence but have to rely on his promises, he is doing a deeper work than we could ever imagine.

Suffering changes us like nothing else can. It draws us to God. It makes us more compassionate and understanding and wise. It produces perseverance and teaches us how to earnestly pray. It reframes our perspective.

Those who have suffered deeply know how to comfort others in their grief. They are less likely to draw straight lines between obedience and blessing because they understand the mystery in suffering, in life, and in God. There are no easy answers with grief, and pretending to have them can seem superficial at best and cruel at worst. God and his ways are inscrutable, and often we need to leave it at that without offering trite explanations.

No one can understand or explain another's suffering. Just as I cannot fully understand or explain my own. I simply must trust that he is using all things for my good. To engage me rather than alienate me. To prosper me, not to harm me. To give me a hope and a future.

Without the Lord, these past twenty years would have made me bitter. Twenty years that have seen the death of my son, a debilitating disease, and a dissolved marriage, among other trials. But these twenty years have brought a closeness to Christ, an unshakeable joy, and a keener awareness of my sin. And because of Jesus, those blessings will ultimately far outweigh all the pain.

My life has vacillated between glorious sunshine and terrible downpours. I have never known how long any of those times would last. But I do know that while I love the sunlight, I need the rain because it does the deepest work in my life. I do not wish a pain-free life on anyone I love. A pain-free life is not a blessing. A pain-free life yields little of lasting value. The rain God sends does indeed demonstrate his faithfulness.

So I want to tell my dear friend:

> I understand how you feel. These relentless trials may make you feel that God doesn't care, or doesn't love you. Nothing could be further from the truth. Even though God may feel far away, he is nearer now than he has ever been.
>
> He is doing things in your life that will amaze you when you are able to step back and look at them. This torrential downpour in your life is a sign of his love.
>
> The rain God sends does indeed demonstrate his faithfulness to you.

PART III: JOY COMES WITH THE MORNING

*Weeping may tarry for the night, but
joy comes with the morning.
(Psalm 30:5)*

THE LENS OF THANKSGIVING

Living life with gratitude has not come easily for me.

I know I should count my blessings, but sometimes it's just easier to count my miseries. It comes more naturally. And miseries capture my thoughts and interrupt my days more readily than blessings. But counting my miseries seems to shrink my soul, and in the end I am more miserable than when I began.

Counting my blessings may be arduous at first—an act of obedience rather than an overflow of joy—but in the end it opens up space in my heart. When I choose to focus on what I have been given, rather than linger on what I'm missing, I feel happier. More content. Less agitated.

And when I choose to face my miseries directly and find blessings in them, something miraculous happens. I view all of life differently. I see my circumstances through a lens of faith. And I am able to declare with confidence that, even in the worst of circumstances, God is still good, and there is much to be thankful for.

The Pilgrims' Perspective

For years I pictured the first Thanksgiving as the Pilgrims' joyful celebration of a bountiful harvest, sharing with the indigenous people God's abundant provision in a fertile new land. But celebrating the first Thanksgiving was an act of faith and worship, not a natural response to prosperity and abundance.

In the fall of 1620, the Mayflower set sail for Virginia with 102 passengers on board. On December 16, they landed in Massachusetts, far north of their intended destination, just as winter was setting in. This northern climate was much harsher than Virginia's, and the settlers were unprepared for the cold season ahead. Winter brought bitter temperatures and rampant sickness. Shelter was rudimentary. Food was scarce. People lay dying.

That winter, all but three families dug graves in the hard New England soil to bury a husband, wife, or child. By the spring of 1621, half the Pilgrims had died from disease and starvation. No one was untouched by tragedy.

And yet in the midst of these monumental losses, the Pilgrims chose to give thanks. They saw in Scripture that the Israelites had thanked God in all their circumstances. Even before provision and deliverance came, the Israelites were instructed to give thanks. King Jehoshaphat saw the power of thanksgiving as the Israelites' enemies were routed before their eyes while they were praising God (2 Chronicles 20). And the words they used were similar to the beautiful refrain that runs through so many Psalms, "Oh give thanks to the Lord, for he is good; for his steadfast love endures forever!" (Ps. 118:1).

The Pilgrims and Israelites chose to be grateful for what they had, rather than to focus on all they had lost. They had to look for blessings, actively and deliberately. Their thanksgiving was not based on pleasant circumstances but rather on the understanding that God was to be thanked in both prosperity and adversity. Their gratitude was not a "positive thinking" façade, but a deep and steadfast trust that God was guiding all their circumstances, even when life was difficult. Viewing their lives through a lens of gratitude changed their perspective.

I have found that viewing life through a lens of gratitude can change everything.

Choose Your Focus

A close friend of mine is a photographer. She sees things I would never notice. We can drive by an old, faded barn, and I see a dilapidated building in need of paint while she sees a beautifully weathered structure with great character. She focuses on unique angles and lines, observing intricate details that don't even register with me. She's willing to look past the obvious and relish the small things. My friend ends up with breathtaking photos of scenery that I would have completely overlooked. All because of what she chooses to focus her lens on.

In the same way, how I view my own life is dependent on what I choose to focus on. From some angles it looks like a mess. But from other vantages, it is beautiful. My perspective all depends on where I direct my lens.

Several years ago, when I was diagnosed with post-polio syndrome, I was devastated. The doctors told me that my diagnosis meant setting aside the way of life I was accustomed to and starting a whole new life. A life where I did less and rested more. A life where my arms were to be used for essentials—no painting, no scrapbooking, no cooking. A life where dependence on others was necessary and independence was a thing of the past.

This new life was excruciating. I didn't ask for it and I certainly didn't want it. I saw nothing to be thankful for. All around me was loss. It seemed that everything I loved doing had been taken away. Connecting with people, showing hospitality, creating beauty—these were what had inspired me. And all of those outlets were gone. I was pitiful, miserable, and disconsolate.

Yet it was out of this challenging loss that my online writing began. In the same week, three separate friends encouraged me to start writing. They all felt led to tell me after prayer. So I prayed about it as well. And God seemed to confirm their words. I had never aspired to be a writer. I certainly didn't feel gifted as one. Up until then, my only writing had been in my private journal with the Lord.

But nonetheless, I started writing online in December 2013, mainly out of obedience. It didn't require physical effort since I could use voice-activated software to get my words on the screen. I could do it at my own pace if I was exhausted. And I could connect with others without ever leaving my home. It has been a tremendous blessing and privilege to share with people what God has taught me in the darkness.

I would never have chosen this path myself, and from certain angles my life looks bleak. Yet from other angles it is beautiful. I see God using me. I am grateful for all he's done in my life. And I am excited about the future. When I view my life with the lens of thanksgiving, I can see how much I have to be grateful for.

I don't know what the future holds for me—or for you—but I can promise you this: The one who holds you is guiding all your circumstances. And for that assurance, we can all be thankful.

EVER ON DISPLAY

The angels and demons are constantly watching to see how we treasure God.

When I initially heard this idea, it changed me radically. At first it was unsettling to think that I was constantly being watched. Yet it became strangely comforting when I realized I was not alone in my suffering. That there was a greater purpose to my being faithful than I could see.

The Value of Unseen Suffering

Over the years, I had often wondered if my private suffering had much meaning. I understood that Christlike suffering, such as the faithfulness of the martyrs, inspired believers and unbelievers to see the value of God. But unseen suffering that no one else on earth was aware of seemed pointless. Or at least it seemed pointless to me.

If no one ever knew what I was going through, how could God use it? If it didn't inspire others to love Jesus more, did it really matter? If no one was there to observe it, what was the point of a godly response?

And yet as I heard John Piper unpack the book of Job, I saw that my response to suffering mattered. Not just for me, but because a watching world, a world I could neither see nor hear, was waiting to see how I would respond to trials.

The book of Job begins in the throne room of God. Satan is mocking God, claiming that Job treasures him for what he, Job, has been given. Satan claims that if God takes away what Job has been leaning on, Job will curse God to his face. In essence he implies, "God, Job doesn't really love *you*. He loves your blessings. He worships you not for who you are but for what you give him."

This is a great assault on God's value. And after the worst has happened to Job, Job's wife falls into despair and tells Job to curse God and die. This appears to be a great victory for Satan. Perhaps the demons were raising their arms in celebration. At this point, Piper conjectures that ten thousand angels were watching in dismay, wondering what Job would say as well. But when they hear Job declare, "Shall we receive good from God, and shall we not receive evil?" (Job 2:10), we can imagine twenty thousand angelic arms going up, with voices proclaiming, "Yes, Job! God is more valuable than your health. Thank you for holding fast!"

God's glory is on display for the angels and demons when people demonstrate that their hearts are satisfied in God alone rather than in his gifts. When we declare that God is more precious than our health, our happiness, even our very lives, we highlight his supreme worth to an immense, invisible audience.

That message helped me through years of struggle.

I speak and write about suffering, and sometimes my words inadvertently make it sound wistful and romantic. Almost noble. Talking about "crying myself to sleep" sounds a lot more beautiful than what it really is—feeling nauseated in a dark, lonely room, with an empty box of Kleenex and a raging headache from sobbing.

There's nothing even remotely appealing about raw pain. When no one sees or knows or even seems to care. When morning brings a cold numbness that permeates your soul and makes you feel completely dead inside. When every day seems harder than the day before, and you wonder how much longer you can go on. When life seems grueling and gritty and even gruesome, and death seems like it would be a welcome relief.

And yet, in the midst of crushing circumstances, we know something else is going on. Something bigger than we can imagine. Something that puts our pain into a larger context.

The Eyes of Our Unseen Audience

My life isn't just about me. It's about God and his glory. And because of that, my response matters. Even when it seems that no one on earth is watching. Because there are beings in the heavenlies ever watching. And most importantly, God is watching.

Ephesians 3:10 says, "through the church the manifold wisdom of God might now be made known to the rulers and authorities in the heavenly places." So God's intent is that through the church—you and me—his wisdom will be made known to the powers and principalities in the heavenly realms. The angels and demons learn things about God through watching us respond to affliction.

The spirit world is looking on when we hold our tongue, even though we're tempted to speak unkindly. When we lie suffering in an empty room and no one even knows. When we want to curse God and die and yet choose to bless God and live.

Joni Eareckson Tada's message at a recent women's conference addressed this very topic. Joni, who is a quadriplegic, had been lying awake in bed at 2:00 a.m., nauseated from chemo and wondering if it was all worth it. But suddenly she realized,

> Something dynamic and electrifying is abuzz in my dark room. The unseen world in the spirit realm and all the heavenly hosts including powers and principalities, they're watching me. They are listening to me. And as I respond, they are learning about God and his character through me—little me.
>
> I can't tell you how many times I've been able to press on because I know my life is on display. . . . We don't suffer for nothing and we never suffer alone. . . . My response to hardship is never isolated. It is not true that no one cares or notices. The stakes are high and God's reputation is on the line. It's all for God's glory.
>
> When the spirit world sees God's strong arms hold you in your weakness, the Father gets the glory. The spirit world watches us persevere under pressure and you know what they think? "Oh, how great her God must be to inspire such loyalty through such suffering."[27]

Joni's talk reminded me afresh that my life is being lived before an untold number of beings. Every day I have the opportunity to show the surpassing value of Christ to the unseen watching world.

I can glorify God when I am unfairly accused and choose to respond with grace. When I am worried about a loved one and choose not to fear. When I am wracked with physical or emotional pain and choose to praise God anyway. These choices all matter. Because a heavenly host is watching. Not to judge or condemn us. But to see if our God is worth worshiping. If he is worth living for. And even more, if he is worth dying for.

So let us press on. Fight with joy. Be faithful. Our lives are ever on display.

GRACE ALWAYS HEALS DEEPER

Joni Eareckson Tada's devotional, *Beside Bethesda*, begins with this dedication: "For my pain-pal friends I've met by the pool of Bethesda. With each devotional in this book, I pray for them. . . . These friends, like me, deal daily with pain. Together we are discovering that grace always heals deeper."[28]

Grace always heals deeper. These words hit me hard. I understand the truth behind them. For most of us, "grace always heals deeper" is a sweet idea, but we'd prefer the physical healing. Or emotional healing. Or the return of our wayward child. Or reversal of a financial disaster. Those things are tangible. And visible. A cause for celebration.

But grace. That's an invisible healing. To an outsider, nothing looks different. Life still looks shattered and God may seem uninvolved. But that's just to the casual observer. In reality, we are profoundly changed.

Grace gives us the courage to face anything, healed from the inside out. For this healing is not just for this life but for the next. It is Spirit-breathed, not humanly understandable. It is permanent, not temporary.

Cause to Cry Out

Nonetheless, I still beg God for the temporary healing of this life. And I have done that for decades. The first time I remember doing that was in third grade. Everyone was playing dodgeball while I was sitting on the sidelines, watching. As I always did. I had heard in church that if you have faith and don't doubt, you can ask for anything. So I asked, "God, please, please heal me now. Right now, in front of my class. If you do, I'll do anything you want."

Then I boldly got up and walked across the gym, fully expecting to walk without a limp. But after a few steps, I realized that my limp was unchanged and my small faith was squashed. And I gave up on God. I hadn't prayed much before, but that day I concluded that God wasn't real.

Decades later, I begged God not to take the life of my son. Hours after my prayer, I held his lifeless body in the emergency room. God had not brought the healing I had pleaded for. Years after that, I begged God to bring my husband back. When he left our family, I was devastated. I felt certain that God would eventually restore our family. So I waited and prayed. But restoration never came.

God answered no to each of these requests for healing. Each time, I couldn't understand why. I had asked for good things and had promised to glorify God when they were answered. In the third grade, I became angry and disillusioned. I questioned God's love for me. And I walked away. Later, as a Christ-follower, I had a different response. Though the no was still excruciating, I kept talking to God. I couldn't walk away.

At times my devotional life felt hollow. It seemed like those who got the happy ending were God's favorites. And I was somehow a lesser child because I didn't receive what I wanted.

Or so I thought. I did not know that as God denied each request, he was doing something much deeper in my life. Every day I had to cry out to God for mercy. Every day I had to ask the Spirit for strength. Every day I had to cling to Jesus. Because there was nowhere else to turn and nothing else to cling to.

I read and I prayed and I journaled and I wept. Every day. Day by day, I learned to lean into Christ. And as I learned, he poured grace into me. Grace to accept his plans for my life. Grace to receive his power in my weakness. Grace to see this greater healing. For grace always heals deeper.

Greater, Deeper, Better

My grace-saturated healing is not superficial. It is deep and enduring. It cannot be stolen by adverse circumstances. It has led to an abiding joy in God that I wouldn't exchange for anything.

Joni goes on to say in *Beside Bethesda,* "Somehow, in the midst of your suffering, the Son of God beckons you into the inner sanctum of his own suffering—a place of mystery and privilege you will never forget. I have suffered, yes. But I wouldn't trade places with anybody in the world to be this close to Jesus."[29]

From a woman who struggles daily with quadriplegia and chronic pain and has also survived breast cancer, that almost sounds crazy. But the more I have suffered, the more I understand her words.

Joni recounts the day she and her husband, Ken, were at the pool of Bethesda in Jerusalem. Many times she had pictured that pool and wondered why Jesus had passed her by for healing. Yet that day in Jerusalem, Joni suddenly saw things quite differently.

She writes,

> "Thank You", I whispered. "Thank You for the healing you gave me. The deeper healing. Oh, God, you were so wise in not giving me a physical healing. Because that 'no' meant 'yes' to a stronger faith in you, a deeper prayer life, and a greater understanding of your word. It has purged sin from my life, forced me to depend on your grace, and increased my compassion for others who hurt. It has stretched my hope, given me a lively, buoyant trust in you, stirred an excitement about heaven, and pushed me to give thanks in times of sorrow. It has increased my faith and helped me to love you more. Jesus, I love you more."
>
> He didn't give me the physical healing I had wanted, but the deeper healing I needed so much more.[30]

God invites us all to experience this deeper healing. This miracle of a changed heart rather than changed circumstances. This healing that strengthens our prayer life, increases our faith, and helps us love Jesus more. This healing that is not shallow or fleeting; it will last throughout eternity.

For grace always heals deeper.

SUFFERING IS A GIFT

Can trials be a blessing? They certainly didn't feel like blessings when I was in the midst of them, but as I reflect back, I realize they were the making of my faith.

God vividly demonstrated that truth to me through a discussion with some friends who had been long-time ministry leaders. Years earlier, they had gone to a conference to help them discern where the Lord was leading them. At the conference, they were each given a large piece of paper and asked to chart a timeline of their life's high and low points. They later connected these points into a graph that had great peaks, signifying moments of accomplishment and times of pure delight, and valleys representing painful loss, rejection, and loneliness.

After reflection on what was going on in these peaks and valleys, the counselor then turned their graphs upside down. He said, "This is God's perspective on your high points and low points. It's the opposite of your perspective. *God sees our lowest moments as our spiritual highs because that is when he is doing the deepest work in us.* And it is out of those valleys that God gives us our platform for ministry. These low points are essential for us as we discern our calling and our walk with Christ. From them come our most significant growth and our greatest dependence on God."

From our lowest emotional points comes our most significant growth. Our greatest dependence on God. Our platform for ministry. It is in these low points that God does his deepest work in us.

Flip the Graph

Of course. How simple, yet how profound. I'd known that we are shaped by our trials, but doing the simple exercise for myself made it so much clearer.

When I first looked at the graph as I had drawn it, before I turned it upside down, seeing the low points reminded me how agonizing they were. How they seemed to last forever. How they left me feeling lonely and abandoned. It honestly didn't feel like God was doing anything worthwhile in my life as I struggled with doubt, fear, and anger. God often felt distant as I wondered why he didn't answer my prayers.

Looking at the high points on the graph made me smile. I could see God's hand in them. I saw answers to my prayers, fulfillment of my dreams, satisfaction in my work. They were definitely times of joy and abundance. While they were not times of deep spiritual growth, they were times of thankfulness. They were important and life-giving, for without them, I might have fallen into despair.

Turning the graphs upside down revealed a completely different picture. It so beautifully depicted how God's perspective is wholly different than mine. The previous valleys became the mountaintops. The times that felt agonizing and painful taught me to trust God and to lean into him. They became the basis of my ministry. They were often turning points in my life as they trained me to walk by faith and not sight.

The previous mountaintop events were not actually my spiritual low points—while flipping over the graph is helpful, I don't want to push the technique too far—but those peak times were often seasons of self-focus. While I was grateful for the ways God had blessed me in the peaks, I needed to guard against becoming self-congratulatory and proud of those events.

Value the Valleys

I often reflect back on that exercise when I'm struggling. Because when I'm in the pit, I'd like to eliminate all the valleys on my graph. I'd be thrilled if the line of my life story featured frequent upward peaks—times of success and fulfillment—but otherwise be mostly flat. That way there would be no more valleys, no more anguish or tears or pain. Just happiness. And that sounds wonderful.

But turning that graph around, I would see a boring, unexamined, and unfruitful spiritual life. An untested life marked by superficiality and entitlement. A life filled with temporary happiness but little lasting joy.

Suffering and trials are gifts. They refine my character, draw me to God, deepen my faith. They have shaped my theology and carved into me the capacity for great joy. In many ways they are God's greatest blessings.

Years ago, I was talking to a friend who had experienced few trials in life. She was financially prospering, had a solid marriage, and enjoyed good health and obedient, loving children. By her own admission, her life lacked for nothing. But then she talked about the struggles that she had in her faith. God seemed distant and vague to her. She envied those who had been through suffering because of the way it transformed them. They had a passion for God and a fruitfulness in ministry that eluded her. She was sure that there was something in her experience with God that was missing.

We talked about this several times, and I wanted her to see that *feeling* close to God is not the only thing that matters. Sometimes we need to have faith in the dark, without having strong emotions of being drawn to him. Faith is much more about consistently walking with the Lord and trusting him than it is about feeling his presence, or having spiritual "experiences."

But at the same time, I understood what she was saying. Faith seems easier for those who have suffered. It is as though suffering is a strange sort of gift from God, a gift that we reluctantly receive and constantly want to give back. But it has extraordinary power to change us. It changes our outlook, our faith, our walk with God. When we have walked through trials, we are never the same again. Academic learning can be forgotten or discarded, but the lessons we learn from suffering are woven into the fabric of our being. They become part of us.

In the midst of trials, I rarely feel that spiritual growth is happening. Often I'm depressed and just trying to hang on. Life is gray, and I don't see God's work at all. But in retrospect, it is in the hanging on, the trusting in the dark, the waiting patiently for God, where real growth occurs.

I want a life of depth and meaning, a life that reflects Jesus above all else, a life that is marked by faithfulness and joy in him. But those qualities are hard won, and for many of us, to get there we must take the hands of Suffering and

Sorrow, as Much Afraid did in the allegory, *Hinds Feet on High Places.*[31]

The valleys of my life have been lonely and painful, but they have borne fruit that the mountains never could. In those dark valleys, I have learned to trust God. In the end, that has made all the difference.

SUSTAINING GRACE

I walk into Bible study hesitantly. This week we are talking about prayer. I'm not sure how honest I should be. While I see tremendous value in prayer, I've had my own struggles with it. Especially when people talk about their miraculous answers. The ones that happen immediately after they've prayed about something for the first time—when I've prayed about things for years and nothing has changed.

"Some of my prayers have remained unanswered for decades," I offer tentatively. It sounds odd to say this aloud. My evident disappointment seems so unspiritual, so faithless, so shallow.

Scornful of Grace

But then Florence says something that refocuses my attention. Immediately, I know that her words are for me. "You never hear anyone in the Bible complaining about the parting of the Red Sea," she says. "Everyone loves the grace that delivers us. But the Israelites, like us, were dissatisfied with daily manna. We all complain about the grace that merely sustains us."

We all complain about sustaining grace. The truth of it hits me hard. I can scarcely pay attention to the rest of the discussion as I ponder. Were my prayers for *deliverance* answered with the gift of *sustenance*? Do I not see that this was an answer, too? And often just as miraculous? Why am I not grateful for manna? The everyday, sustaining grace of God.

When I later tell Florence how her words are staying with me, how they are changing everything for me, she writes this to me: "I remember being stunned by the realization of how much I love deliverance and how little I appreciate sustenance. Essentially, I was saying 'Where is the victory in sustenance—it sounds like just getting by.' Wasn't I being scornful of grace?"

Scornful of grace. Exactly. I've often been guilty of that.

In waiting for the huge, monumental deliverance— the kind where I can put my issue to bed and never have to pray about it again—I've overlooked the grace that keeps drawing me to him. The prayers that may appear unanswered, but actually are fulfilled in ways that keep me dependent, tethered, needy.

The Gift of Dependence

The children of Israel were familiar with the gift of dependence. Manna dropped from heaven so they wouldn't starve as they wandered in the wilderness (Ex. 16). But they needed God to provide it daily; they weren't able to hoard it. And thus they couldn't avoid total dependence on God.

The Israelites were given bread so that they would rely on God and live by his word. But like me, they often disdained it (Num. 11). Manna was bland, unexciting, monotonous. It wasn't what they asked for. It wasn't extraordinary or gloriously victorious like the parting of the Red Sea

(Ex. 14) or some of the miracles yet to come, like the fall
of Jericho (Josh. 6) or the healing of Naaman (2 Kings 5).
It didn't impress people. Manna simply provided for their
needs when they were in the desert. It became expected.
And taken for granted.

I know how they felt. I often feel that way as well. I
don't appreciate God's unfailing presence throughout the
day. I don't acknowledge that he strengthens me when I
am weak. I overlook the life-giving power of God's word. I
want miraculous deliverance. Not ordinary sustenance.

But as I look back over my life, I see God has delivered me and answered some prayers with a resounding
yes in jaw-dropping, inexplicable ways. I remember those
answers with gratitude and awe. But the answers of "wait"
or "no" have done a far deeper work in my soul. They have
kept me connected to the giver and not his gifts. They have
forced me to seek him. And in seeking him, I have found
a supernatural joy beyond all comparison. A joy not based
on my circumstances. Not based on my deliverance. Simply
based on his tender presence.

Delivering grace or sustaining grace. Which is more
precious?

We Need Both

In delivering grace, we see God's glory. Everyone can see
the miracle he has wrought *for us*. And usually our lives
are easier as a result. We have what we asked for. And we
thank God for it. But after a while, we go back to the busi-
ness of living. New difficulties come up. And we may even
forget about what he's done because we aren't continuously
going back to him.

Sustaining grace also showcases God's glory. But with sustaining grace, people can see the miracle he has wrought *in us*. Our lives are easier because our perspective is different. With sustaining grace, we must continually go back to God. This grace is not a one-time thing, just as manna was not a one-time event. We need it every day. And it keeps us dependent on God. With sustaining grace, we get more of Jesus. His comfort, his nearness, his very presence.

Both delivering grace and sustaining grace are essential in the Christian life. They are interconnected. Delivering grace is vital. We need to pray for it. It's biblical. Life can be relentlessly hard, and we need to know that deliverance is possible. That our prayers are effective. That our situation can change. Without the possibility of deliverance, we'd lose hope. We might stop praying. We could succumb to total despair.

But it is in the asking, even begging, for deliverance, and in the subsequent waiting for it, that we get sustaining grace, the grace to press on in the blazing heat. And this grace is accompanied by the intimate presence of the living God. So when I am sustained but not delivered, God is inviting me to see the miracle I have received. It is a more precious answer to prayer than I ever realized.

Manna, my daily bread, the Bread of Life himself. He alone sustains me in the desert.

THE STAGGERING PROMISE OF HEAVEN

I'm listening to a speaker, and she's talking about a difficult period in her life. Years when her prayers seemed unanswered and God felt distant and uncaring. Years when she gave up and even stopped praying. Years when nothing seemed to change.

I am immediately drawn into her story because I understand how that feels. I remember feeling as if I were drowning, wondering if I would ever come up for air. Gasping for breath, hanging on, surviving—but just barely. It was almost a decade before I could breathe deeply again.

I am thankful that I was finally able to catch my breath. But not everyone can. There are people who live in anguish day after day, month after month, year after year. And nothing changes. Ever. For them, life on this earth is just one endless struggle after another.

Not in This Life

On a smaller scale, many of us deal with some specific personal struggle that will never go away. The death of a loved one tears a gaping hole in our heart. An irreversible, debilitating disease reminds us daily of our mortality. Chronic depression ambushes us when we least expect, bringing with it desperation and inertia. Rebellious children, difficult marriages, divorce, financial ruin, loneliness, regret. Some of this pain will never get better. Not in this life.

It all sounds so hopeless, and I'm feeling despair for the millions of people whose lives are marked by pain. I realize my hope often rests in the assumption that things will eventually get better. And I wonder: *If they never do get better, could it all be worth it?*

As I'm pondering that idea, my attention is drawn back to the speaker, and then she says it. The words that change everything. "One day, in heaven, all our longings will be met or will fade away."

Of course. That's it. That's what we need to hold onto. That is the truth worth suffering for, worth living for, and worth dying for.

The Day Everything Changes

Heaven will change everything. Things may or may not get better for us in this life, but one day, one glorious day, everything will be made new. One day, in the blink of an eye, it will all be changed.

Why don't I write more about heaven? I keep asking myself that question. Much as I have been blessed by knowing God on this earth and his comfort and incredible love in the midst of great sorrow, it should pale in comparison to the joys of heaven.

The Bible constantly reminds us that our present sufferings must be viewed in light of eternity. Romans 8:18 says, "I consider that the sufferings of this present time are not worth comparing with the glory that is to be revealed to us."

Paul knew that this life alone would never be able to balance the scales of suffering. But it was never meant to. We were made for heaven, for eternal life. Looking at this life in the context of heaven is the only way to make sense of suffering. Let alone make up for it.

Randy Alcorn asserts:

> Second Corinthians 4:17 . . . says that eternal glo-
> ry far outweighs our worst suffering. It's not that
> temporary suffering is so small; it's that eternal
> glory is so huge. Your suffering may be a boulder
> the size of the Rock of Gibraltar. But suppose
> you put that rock on one side of the scales, then
> on the other side you put the planet Jupiter. In
> and of themselves our sufferings may be weighty,
> but compare them to eternal glory, everlast-
> ing happiness, endless beauty, and unbroken
> relationships. The relative weights change our
> perspective, don't they?[32]

Reading this comparison, I was convicted about my short-sightedness. I need to remind myself why I am here. I was created to glorify God and enjoy him forever—with the overwhelming majority of "forever" not spent on earth. Because of Jesus's death on the cross, I get to spend all of eternity with God in heaven.

Happily Ever After

What a breathtaking truth. I will spend eternity with God in heaven. But often the vastness of that truth escapes me because my picture of heaven is too vague and undefined. I know it will be glorious because God says it will be, but I have not imagined what it will be like. My ideas of heaven are abstract, which makes them less appealing, and sometimes I feel cheated about the joys on earth I may never experience.

That perspective is exactly what Satan wants me to believe. Satan wants us to think that this life holds pleasures that we cannot experience in heaven. That in heaven we will sit on clouds, playing harps, with no physical bodies and no real "fun." That the excitement of this life is better than what heaven offers.

Those are patent lies. The Bible says we will have resurrected bodies. Physical bodies. We will not be spirits or disembodied ghosts. There will be a new, physical heaven; a new, physical earth. God created pleasure and he will maximize it in heaven. Heaven will be incredible because God is incredible.

Alcorn observes:

> He made our taste buds, adrenaline, and the nerve endings that convey pleasure to our brains. Likewise, our imaginations and capacity for joy were made by . . . God. . . . Are we so arrogant as to imagine that human beings came up with the idea of having fun?
>
> When Christians understand heaven is an exciting physical place on a redeemed world with redeemed people in redeemed relationships without sin and death, where there is music, art, science, sports, literature, and culture, it's a great source of encouragement and motivation.[33]

This life-giving perspective encourages me to anticipate heaven. Everything I love and long for on earth will be there, only better. And it will more than make up for any suffering I've experienced on earth. Life on this earth can be relentlessly hard, and we may live with unending pain. But because of the gospel, God has all of eternity to lavish his love on us. In heaven there will be no more tears or crying or pain.

As Alcorn says, "'They all lived happily ever after' is not merely a fairy tale. It's the blood-bought promise of God for all who trust in the gospel."[34]

God's blood-bought promise for those who trust in the gospel is that we will live happily ever after in heaven. What a staggering assurance. And a glorious future.

ACKNOWLEDGMENTS

Joel, my beloved husband, you have brought unimaginable joy to my life and shown me the goodness of God in ways I cannot express.

Katie and Kristi, you are amazing daughters and I love watching you both grow in your faith, rejoicing over the beauty of Christ in you.

Dad, Mom, and Shalini, you gave me my first taste of unconditional love and have been unfailing anchors throughout my life.

Jennifer and Lisa, my faithful prayer partners, you have supported me in untold ways during our 20 years of praying together.

Christ Covenant Church, you have pointed me to our glorious God as we have worshiped together.

The readers of my blog, you stayed with me as I struggled to find my voice, supported me along the way, and entrusted me with your precious stories.

The staff at Desiring God, particularly John Piper, who taught me to see God in all my suffering, and David Mathis, who suggested I write this book and encouraged me throughout the process.

There are countless people who have mentored me, knowingly and unknowingly, throughout the years. I wish

I could thank each of you here, for I have been shaped by your words and your lives.

I owe a debt of gratitude to all of you. Thank you.

ENDNOTES

1. Based on a line from the poem *Joseph's Coat* by George Herbert.
2. Michael Card, "Known by the Scars," in *Known by the Scars*, Sparrow Records, 1983.
3. "Scar," Dictionary.com. http://www.dictionary.com/browse/scar. Accessed June 21, 2016.
4. Content largely drawn from "I Was Bullied as a Child," first published September 10, 2014 in *Today's Christian Woman* (part of *Christianity Today*). http://www.todayschristianwoman.com/articles/2014/september-week-2/i-was-bullied-as-child.html. Accessed October 4, 2016.
5. Christa Wells, "Held," Weimarhymes Publishing, Inc., 2001.
6. Content largely drawn from "The Hardest Thing to Ask For," first published January 7, 2015 in *Today's Christian Woman* (part of *Christianity Today*). http://www.todayschristianwoman.com/articles/2015/january-week-1/hardest-thing-to-ask-for.html. Accessed 10/4/2016.
7. Content largely drawn from "From Wailing to Worship," first published April 5, 2016 in *Today's Christian Woman* (part of *Christianity Today*). http://www.christianitytoday.com/women/2016/april/from-wailing-to-worship.html. Accessed 10/4/2016.

8. Laura Story, "Blessings," in *Blessings*, New Spring, 2011.

9. Attributed to Reverend John Watson, who went by the pseudonym Ian MacLaren c. 1897.

10. D. Martyn Lloyd-Jones, *Spiritual Depression: Its Causes and Cures* (Grand Rapids, MI: Eerdmans, 1965), 20.

11. Caroline Lusk, "Storytelling: Laura Story finds blessings in the story gone different." *CCM Magazine*, 7 May 2011.

12. Edward Mote, "My Hope is Built on Nothing Less," *Hymns of Praise*. 1836.

13. Paul Tripp, "God's Will for Your Wait (part 2)," *Paul Tripp Ministries*, May 27, 2013. http://www.paultripp.com/articles/posts/gods-willfor-your-wait-part-two. Accessed June 27, 2016.

14. John Newton, *The Letters of John Newton* (Edinburgh: Banner of Truth, 1960), 180, quoted in Timothy Keller, *Walking with God Through Pain and Suffering* (New York: Penguin Group, 2013), 266.

15. Charles Spurgeon, "The Simplicity and Sublimity of Salvation," delivered June 5, 1892.

16. This is popularly attributed to Charles Spurgeon, but the author has been unable to identify a source.

17. Arthur Bennet, "The Valley of Vision." *The Valley of Vision: A Collection of Puritan Prayers and Devotions* (Edinburgh: Banner of Truth, 2003), xxv.

18. Joni Eareckson Tada, Foreword to *Choosing Gratitude: Your Journey to Joy* by Nancy Leigh DeMoss (Chicago: Moody Publishers, 2009), 12.

19. Joni Eareckson Tada and Steve Estes, *When God Weeps: Why Our Sufferings Matter to the Almighty*

(Grand Rapids: Zondervan, 1997), 56, 56, 84, 84, 101, 137.

20. Joni Eareckson Tada, *The God I Love* (Grand Rapids: Zondervan, 2003), 357.

21. George Matheson quoted in L. B. Cowman, *Streams in the Desert* (Grand Rapids: Zondervan, 1996), 114.

22. Alexander Solzhenitsyn, *The Gulag Archipelago: 1918–1956, Vol. 2*, 615–617 quoted by John Piper, "Thank You, Lord, for Solzhenitsyn," in Desiring God, August 4, 2008. http://www.desiringgod.org/articles/thank-you-lord-for-solzhenitsyn. Accessed June 28, 2016.

23. Joni Eareckson Tada, foreword to *Choosing Gratitude: Your Journey to Joy* by Nancy Leigh DeMoss (Chicago: Moody Publishers, 2009), 12.

24. Joseph Bayly, *The View from a Hearse* (Colorado Springs: David C. Cook Publishing, 1972) 40.

25. John Wyatt, *Matters of Life and Death* (Downers Grove: InterVarsity Press, 2009).

26. D. A. Carson, *How Long, O Lord?: Reflections on Suffering and Evil* (Grand Rapids: Baker Academic, 1990), 109.

27. Joni Eareckson Tada, "The Stakes Are Higher than You Think," (presentation, True Woman Conference, Indianapolis, IN, September 24, 2010).

28. Joni Eareckson Tada, *Beside Bethesda: 31 Days Toward Deeper Healing* (Carol Stream: NavPress, 2016), Dedication.

29. Ibid., 81.

30. Ibid., 168.

31. Hannah Hurnard, *Hinds' Feet on High Places* (Carol Stream: Tyndale, 1975).

32. Randy Alcorn, "C. S. Lewis on Heaven and the New Earth: God's Eternal Remedy to the Problem of Evil and Suffering," *Desiring God*, September 28, 2013, accessed June, 21, 2016. http://www.desiringgod.org/messages/c-s-lewis-on-heaven-and-the-new-earth-god-s-eternal-remedy-to-the-problem-of-evil-and-suffering.

33. Randy Alcorn, interview by Gavin Ortlund, "Looking Forward to a Heaven We Can Imagine," *The Gospel Coalition*, March 9, 2015. https://www.thegospelcoalition.org/article/lookingforward-to-a-heaven-we-can-imagine. Accessed June 21, 2016.

34. Ibid.

❊ desiringGod

Everyone wants to be happy. Our website was born and built for happiness. We want people everywhere to understand and embrace the truth that God is most glorified in us when we are most satisfied in him. We've collected more than thirty years of John Piper's speaking and writing, including translations into more than forty languages. We also provide a daily stream of new written, audio, and video resources to help you find truth, purpose, and satisfaction that never end. And it's all available free of charge, thanks to the generosity of people who've been blessed by the ministry.

If you want more resources for true happiness, or if you want to learn more about our work at Desiring God, we invite you to visit us at www.desiringGod.org.

---

www.desiringGod.org

Made in the USA
San Bernardino, CA
17 December 2016